D0720065

Retired broke

Retired Broke

HOW TO FIX YOUR RETIREMENT

Randy Kirk and Jane Kirk

Fugal Frog Enterprises, LLC
Retired Broke: How to Fix Your Retirement
By Randy Kirk and Jane Kirk, HIA, ALHC

Editor: Kelly Lamb
Cover Design by RacDesign.concept@gmail.com
Cover Image copyright VirtualImage, used under license from Shutterstock.com
Randy & Jane Kirk photograph by Tasha Schriever, Beauty of Life Photography Studio.

Published in the United States by Frugal Frog Enterprises, LLC.
ISBN: 0990943801
ISBN 9780990943808
Library of Congress Control Number: 2014922481
Frugal Frog Enterprises, LLC, Olathe, KS

Version 1.1 (Charleston, SC)
Printed by CreateSpace

Contents

Disclaimer · vii

Acknowledgments · ix

Introduction: When You Don't Have Enough Saved
for Your Golden Years · xi

Part I ·1

Take an Assessment: Where Are You Now?
Where Are You Going? ·1

Part II ·6

Drastically Reduce Your Overhead ·6

Housing· ·6

Health Care: The Cost of Staying Healthy · · · · · · · · · · · · · · · · · ·17

Transportation ·25

Food ·28

Insurance $\cdots\cdots\cdots\cdots\cdots\cdots\cdots\cdots\cdots\cdots\cdots\cdots$ 29

Taxes $\cdots\cdots\cdots\cdots\cdots\cdots\cdots\cdots\cdots\cdots\cdots\cdots\cdots$ 33

Debt $\cdots\cdots\cdots\cdots\cdots\cdots\cdots\cdots\cdots\cdots\cdots\cdots\cdots$ 35

Having Fun with Entertainment, Hobbies, Traveling, and Pets $\cdots\cdots\cdots\cdots\cdots\cdots\cdots\cdots\cdots\cdots$ 39

Bad Habits $\cdots\cdots\cdots\cdots\cdots\cdots\cdots\cdots\cdots\cdots\cdots$ 41

Miscellaneous $\cdots\cdots\cdots\cdots\cdots\cdots\cdots\cdots\cdots\cdots$ 43

Charity $\cdots\cdots\cdots\cdots\cdots\cdots\cdots\cdots\cdots\cdots\cdots\cdots$ 45

Part III $\cdots\cdots\cdots\cdots\cdots\cdots\cdots\cdots\cdots\cdots\cdots\cdots$ 46

Income Options $\cdots\cdots\cdots\cdots\cdots\cdots\cdots\cdots\cdots\cdots$ 46

Earning Income from Your Investments $\cdots\cdots\cdots\cdots$ 46

Part-Time Work $\cdots\cdots\cdots\cdots\cdots\cdots\cdots\cdots\cdots\cdots$ 53

Starting a Business on a Shoestring $\cdots\cdots\cdots\cdots\cdots$ 55

How It's Done: Examples $\cdots\cdots\cdots\cdots\cdots\cdots\cdots$ 59

Conclusion $\cdots\cdots\cdots\cdots\cdots\cdots\cdots\cdots\cdots\cdots\cdots$ 67

Appendix: How to Avoid the 10 Percent Penalty from an IRA Withdrawal $\cdots\cdots\cdots\cdots\cdots\cdots\cdots\cdots\cdots$ 69

Bibliography $\cdots\cdots\cdots\cdots\cdots\cdots\cdots\cdots\cdots\cdots\cdots$ 73

About the Authors $\cdots\cdots\cdots\cdots\cdots\cdots\cdots\cdots\cdots$ 75

Disclaimer

The content in this book is for information and entertainment only. The authors are not providing professional investment advisory services and are not rendering legal, accounting, or other professional services. If legal, accounting, or other expert assistance is required, the services of a competent professional should be sought. The authors have not received compensation in any form from any person or company referenced in this book. The authors have made every effort to provide accurate and truthful information in this book. All information is believed to be from reliable sources; however, we make no representations as to the accuracy or completeness of any information in this book or information found by visiting any link presented in this book. Enjoy the book and may your life be fun and fulfilling.

Acknowledgments

Special thanks to our patient and talented editor, Kelly Lamb, for giving guidance during this project.

Thank you to Rachmad Agus Ridwan for expressing your artistic talent.

We are so grateful to the many people that helped us along the way, including Lynn and Peter Lippitt, Macha and John Greenleaf Maple, Brian Kirk, Melinda Kirk, Laurie Farnsworth, and Suzanne Thompson.

Last but not least, we couldn't have done it without you, Mom. Thanks for keeping it all together.

Introduction: When You Don't Have Enough Saved for Your Golden Years

We are a husband and wife writing team with extensive experience in government and the insurance industry. Early retirement was something always on our minds and we would occasionally review the numbers to see when we could make the decision to leave our jobs. We wanted to spend more time together pursuing our hobbies, traveling, and spending time with our grandkids.

Finally, we both retired early, about three years ago, in our fifties. Was it a mistake? Unexpected expenses and inflation experienced during our short retirement made a big dent in our nest egg. The 18% yearly increases to our health insurance premiums were especially damaging to our budget. This was unsustainable and we worried that we might run out of money before our time was up if this continued. Instead of going back to work full time we decided to find another way to cope with an underfunded retirement. This book contains steps we have researched—many of which we have taken ourselves—that can make a difference in your retirement.

There seems to be a great number of people in underfunded retirements. Maybe you are one of them. Perhaps you want to retire, but you're basically broke. You don't have to be completely without money to have an unsuccessful retirement. A partially funded retirement is still considered retired broke, because your savings probably won't last as long as your retirement years. One-third of folks aged fifty-five to sixty-four in 2010 had no savings to finance their retirement. Another third of retirees had only managed to save a median figure of $100,000 for retirement. For those with no retirement accounts, such as an IRA or 401(k), the median savings was only $40,000. This information comes from a June 2013 study by a non-profit organization, the National Institute on Retirement Security, authored by Nari Rhee, PhD.

This is a crisis. Some of it can be blamed on individuals for not thinking ahead and starting to save their money sooner, but some is attributed to events beyond our control, such as inflation, unexpected medical bills, and suppressed wages.

Maybe you've been forced into early retirement because someone half-way across the globe will do your job cheaper or because a machine took your position. You may have some money saved, but you know it will not be enough to finance your retirement for the next twenty-five to thirty years. Maybe you can keep working a few more years at your present job, if you have one, or go back to work full time at another job. But who will hire you? Nobody wants to admit it, but age discrimination in the workplace exists.

Our theme here is to drastically cut expenses without sacrificing a comfortable living. Big-dollar items, such as housing, transportation, and health care, are examined for potential savings that can make a big impact on your budget. We also discuss how to generate income if needed. We look into casual income from part-time work, starting your own small business for less than $500, ways to best invest what savings you may have, how to tap into your 401(k) or IRA before age fifty-nine and a half without paying a 10 percent penalty, and other creative ways to generate income.

Some of the ideas we examine are extreme or drastic. For example, there is a section on how to live out of your vehicle to help you get back on your feet financially and set up a solid retirement plan. Other ideas are perhaps easier to envision, such as simply renting out the spare bedroom(s) you have in your house or apartment. You make the choice depending on the severity of your situation. You do not have to follow every step in the book; just select the ideas you feel comfortable with based on your situation.

This book will show you how to fix your retirement. The creative steps outlined may guide you toward peace of mind, and you may actually enjoy your golden years. At least you'll be able to keep a roof over your head and food in your pantry.

INTRODUCTION: WHEN YOU DON'T HAVE ENOUGH SAVED...

There are four ways to fix a broken retirement:

- Increase your savings. If you have the time and means to earn cash, start socking away a large percentage of it. (However, you may have already missed that boat.)
- Be aggressive with your investments. (Be careful, though. Take too many risks, and you might lose what little savings you do have.)
- Decrease your expenses. If you are willing to make sacrifices, this is the easiest way to fix your retirement.
- Find ways to earn additional income during retirement.

In this book, we concentrate on the last two ways. Reducing your overhead is the most effective and powerful way to fix your retirement, and we will spend a large percentage of time showing you how to do just that.

Substantially reducing your expenses is like having money in the bank. Let's examine how it works. Let's say you retired with no savings, like a third of retirees, but wish you had an annual income of $20,000 from a nest egg. It would require $500,000 in savings to generate that $20,000 income in the first year of retirement. That's taking 4 percent of your nest egg balance to pay expenses each year; the withdrawal rate that most financial advisors recommend. Now, do the math backward. Instead of generating that amount, you find creative ways to reduce your budgeted expenses by $20,000, which has the same effect as having that half a million in the bank.

You could start small. Just remember that every $4,000 you cut from your budget is like having $100,000 in savings in the bank. You find the multiple you want. For example, maybe you already have $200,000 saved for your nest egg but wish you had at least $400,000. If you don't have enough time to build toward that goal, then you simply cut $8,000 from your budget to achieve the same outcome.

Let's say you're really ambitious, and you want to have the same income you would receive from a $500,000 portfolio. We are going to show you how you can cut up to $20,000 from your budget in the following chapters. Impossible, you may say, but anything is possible if you are willing to do what it takes. If you are spending $60,000 a year, instead you will spend $40,000 to maintain your lifestyle. In the event that you are unable to cut that much from your budget, there is a section in the book that will show you how to close the gap by earning additional income during your retirement.

If you manage to cut enough from your budget, you might have enough excess funds from your retirement income, such as Social Security and pensions, to start a savings plan and add to your nest egg during your retirement, which will make for a more secure future.

This book is comprised of three parts:

First, assess your situation. Where are you in your life at this moment? What do you have to work with? Where are you heading?

Second, find ways to reduce your overhead. Reduce your personal infrastructure cost, which will enable you to live on less but still live comfortably.

Third, look at ways to bring money into your life. This could mean getting a part-time job, starting your own small business, or safely investing the nest egg you may have in order to live off the investment income.

We will give an example that shows how a typical couple followed the steps in this book to cut $20,000 from their annual budget. We also show in a second example how someone with only Social Security income survives, and enjoys retirement.

Let's get started.

Part I

Take an Assessment: Where Are You Now? Where Are You Going?

How bad is it? Are you part of the group that is unprepared for retirement? Maybe you just lost your job or your poor health prevents you from working. You're sitting there with little or no savings, maybe with no pension, and you also have some debt. Anxiety may well up inside, and you're unsure of what the future will hold. Can you live on just Social Security if that's all you have? Can you find another source of income to support yourself? Perhaps you're lucky, and it's not that bad. Maybe you do have some savings and are still working, but you still feel like you are unprepared for retirement. What is the first step toward a secure retirement if you are on shaky ground? Take an assessment.

One major reason for anxiety is not knowing where you are or where you are going. Most are winging it as they go along. A written plan is crucial. Yes, that's right; we're asking you to write out your goals on paper, to identify what resources you have available to you to achieve those goals, and to start discovering what creative options may solve your problems. This is what taking an assessment is all about.

The first step is to get a pad of paper and a pen and write down your idea of retirement. Use the whole page; fill it with your dreams. Be fearless—nothing is off-limits when you are describing your vision of what retirement holds for you (and your spouse if you're married). Do you see yourself traveling? Auditioning for the local community theater's production of *A Midsummer Night's Dream*? Perhaps you want to move to be closer to your grandkids. Maybe you want to spend more time pursuing a hobby.

Write down everything you desire. For example, you want to buy an antique sports car to fix up, or you want to take an art class every week at your local college. List every item that will make your retirement match the vision you see in your head. Some of the things you may want are one-time expenditures and could cost quite a bit of money, such as that sports car. Some of the other items are recurring expenses, such as those weekly art classes.

How will you pay for all of your dreams? Are your goals reasonable? You didn't write down that you wanted to fly to Europe every summer in a private jet and live in a $2 million mansion, did you? For some, that might be possible if they earned and saved enough, but let's be realistic: if you're worried about having enough money saved for retirement, you probably aren't in a position to travel lavishly.

You might be happy just to have a roof over your head and groceries in your pantry. So keeping expectations reasonable will make your plan more successful. But wait, that European vacation is something you really, really want. Maybe you can still have it. How? By thinking of creative options, such as exchanging your house for another one in Europe for a few weeks or house-sitting for somebody who lives in London. Now that's thinking outside the box! You could travel to Europe and stay within your modest budget. We cover options for situations like these later in the book.

Speaking of a budget, creating one is our next step. Why budget? Like many, maybe you don't budget. It has never worked, you might say. However, not having a budget is like driving your car at night without the headlights turned on; you can't see what is ahead of you. There might be an unexpected turn in the road that can cause an accident. Having a budget is like turning on the headlights so you can see important things on the horizon. For example, you could discover in January that you don't have enough money to pay your annual car insurance bill, which is due in October. So, you slow down your spending to compensate, like slowing down your car when you see a curve up ahead.

How do you create a savings and spending plan? You can buy budgeting software, use Excel, or take the old-fashioned route with paper and pen. There are even websites that can help you, such as http://www.mint.com, which is an online budgeting tool, or http://www.findfinancialfreedom.org, a site you can use to learn about budgeting and money management.

It really doesn't matter how you keep track of your budget. What's important is that you come up with a system you can work with that will help you achieve your goals. Some like using an Excel spreadsheet, while others keep track with a journal. A budget is something that is personal to you, so make it your own.

The benefits of having a budget are tremendous. Your budget shows you how to allocate your money to avoid debt. It defines spending priorities for your needs and things you enjoy within your financial limitations. It can help you set aside money for emergencies and avoid being caught empty-handed. A budget helps you keep focused on your money goals and see the big picture when you plan for your future. You will be able to see what adjustments you need to make with your life in general. For example, you will be less likely to scramble for money if you have extra funds set aside for large expenditures later in the year, such as that car insurance bill. If you are tempted to spend that extra money that shows up in your checking account, then transfer money to a savings account to be used later. Making monthly payments to yourself in a savings account to pay large-ticket items and cover emergencies will help you manage your money.

Basically, you will be making a list of all the items you plan to spend money on for the year, which reflects the standard of living you are supporting. How much will it cost to keep a roof over your head, and how much will it cost to get around town in your car? What does it cost to stock your refrigerator with food? You should try to list everything. Don't forget to list taxes and the payments you might be making to pay down your credit cards as well as any recurring items that made up the retirement of your dreams in the first exercise. It helps to look at last year's bank and credit card statements to get an idea of how much to budget for the current year. You can also keep a written log for two or three months to get a feel for how you spend your money.

Now you have a yearly budget that shows all of your expenditures. (We will deal with the expensive one-time items on your retirement dream list later.) Don't worry if you don't have enough money to pay for everything.

Next, add all the income you expect to generate in the upcoming year, and compare your grand total to your final budget number. Do you have enough money to cover everything? Most likely you don't. If that's the case, then you have to make some tough decisions. Conventional wisdom says that at this point, you cut what you can't afford from your budget and do without. But what if you can find ways to keep what you can't afford? For example, you can't afford to live in the house you've had for twenty years because taxes and insurance have gone up. Instead of selling your home, you could rent out a bedroom to cover the increased costs. You get to keep your house. Another example of a budget expense you may consider cutting is season tickets to the ballet. You could volunteer to be an usher at the theater and see the ballet shows for free. These are just two examples of creative ways to keep your budget items that might otherwise be cut.

Try to find inventive ways to retain every item on your list that you are considering cutting. Remember, you can also find ways to earn extra income during retirement that might do the trick.

Hopefully, a number of things on your list are free or almost free. Those items most important to you that are not free will find a way to stay in your budget because they will be a priority.

It's important to write or enter your spending transactions each week or month to see if you are on target with your expected expenditures. If you find yourself spending more than you forecast, then you need to adjust your spending or reduce other budget items to add funds to the category in which you are overspending.

If you find keeping track of your transactions on paper or a computer too tedious or unproductive, then another strategy is to use envelopes. You write your budget item, such as groceries, on each envelope. Then, you place cash in each envelope for every budget item for the month. You might have seven or more envelopes. When you need something, take the cash out of the corresponding envelope. When you run out of cash in that particular envelope, then you know you have hit your limit. You might take some money out of another budget envelope if you find yourself in dire straits, but remember, you can't spend more than what you have in all of your envelopes for the month. This way, you can live within your means. You still use your savings account to pay the big-ticket items that appear sporadically during the year. The envelopes are used for your recurring monthly expenses.

If you want to use the envelope method and don't like to keep that much cash around the house, then use your credit cards or write checks and store the receipts in the appropriate budget envelope. For example, put your grocery receipts in your grocery envelope and add them all up at the end of the month to see how well you did. If you are closely watching how much you spend, then adding up your receipts each week should help keep you on track. If you didn't receive a receipt for an item you paid for, then write the transaction on a piece of paper to put in the envelope. This serves as a substitute for a receipt.

What about those items from your retirement dream list that are one-time, costly expenditures? You have to find the money or save up for them. You might have some assets you can sell to offset their cost.

Now is a good time for another exercise. Take a piece of paper and draw a line down the middle. On the left side at the top, write *Assets*. Under *Assets*, list all the items you own and estimate the value for which they can be sold after commissions and other selling costs such as advertising, shipping or perhaps taxes. This includes your house, vehicles, household goods, cash, stocks, bonds, art, and other collectibles.

On the right side at the top, write *Debts*. Simply list the amount of your outstanding loans and credit card balances. Add each column. Subtract the debt total from the asset total. Is it positive, or do you have a negative net worth? This exercise will show if selling some of your possessions to raise cash for the large-ticket items from your dream list would be feasible. Instead, it may be wiser to pay down debt before financing your retirement dreams.

What if you can't find the extra cash or don't have the time and means to save up for your big expenditure items? Try to find ways to do some of the things you think you can't afford to do for less. For example, you have always wanted to travel across the country in an RV for a couple of months a year, but you can't afford the $75,000 rig and all of the associated costs, such as gas, taxes, insurance, RV lot rentals, and so on. It's time to think outside the box. Instead of buying, why not rent an RV for a month and share the experience with friends or family who could pitch in to help pay for the costs? It might be more fun with somebody else tagging along. You also wouldn't have to worry about finding a place to store your RV or paying for all the maintenance, depreciation, and other costs. You could still enjoy the RV experience for a fraction of the cost of owning one. Another idea is to sell your house and live in the RV full time. And then there is always camping in tents if you want to really save money while you travel the country.

The purpose of doing these exercises and making a written plan is to make it possible to see where you are and see where you can go with your retirement life. If you find that you are short of money, then you probably want to consider using some of the ideas in the next two sections of the book. If you find something you can use, then make it part of your written plan.

Part II

Drastically Reduce Your Overhead

The easiest way to take the stress off your budget when money is scarce is to reduce your expenses. The less overhead, the less income is needed. Some of the ideas in this section may seem too drastic for some folks. We offer ideas that we researched and considered for ourselves; you can choose what fits your situation. We found some ideas too far out there. One of us loved the idea of living in a two-hundred-square-foot house, but the other vehemently protested. This solution may be perfect for you, however. If not, there are many other ideas that may be more appealing.

We offer ideas for diminishing or eliminating expenses from your overhead. We've tried to arrange these ideas by the greatest impact to your budget, which is typically housing, health care, transportation, food, insurance, taxes, and debt. The last category is a catchall where we talk about shopping, pets, charity and more.

Housing

Keeping a roof over your head is usually the most expensive component of your budget. If you can reduce the cost of housing, you free up a good chunk of capital to pay for your retirement. It is by far the fastest way to raise cash. For example, the average percentage of income spent on housing in 2013 was almost 27 percent, according to a US Department of Labor survey. If you can reduce your housing cost by half by taking some of the following steps, you will automatically create a windfall close to 14 percent.

You may have heard that downsizing to a smaller house or apartment is the most economical solution, but that is not always the case. You might find that keeping your house can actually save you more money. Your house could become an income-producing asset.

However in some cases, people can come out ahead by downsizing their living space. Staying put or downsizing? Which way will work for you? We cover both options.

Many of the following ideas cannot be utilized by everyone. Each person has his or her own unique situation. One person may have kids, grandkids, or parents living with him or her, which may complicate things. Others need to stay in a particular geographic location for medical or other reasons.

Maybe staying put is the best option

Sometimes, the best thing to do is to stay where you are. Renting out a room or two in your house or apartment is one way to raise cash. Let's say you have two bedrooms rented out for $600 each per month, generating $14,400 per year. That is like having a $360,000 nest egg producing a 4 percent distribution, and it goes up each year adjusted for inflation. Make sure the renters carry their own renter's insurance to cover any losses that could occur. Your homeowner's policy will not pay for your tenant's losses. Don't forget to pay your taxes on this extra income. Remember, depreciation and other expenses will offset the rent income. Approximately one third of your rent receipts is used to pay for maintenance, real estate taxes and insurance. We found a great blog that offers pros and cons and tips for renting to roommates: http://www.rentingoutrooms.com/about.

If you don't like having people sharing your space, then converting a basement, attic, or garage into a small apartment separate from your quarters may be a better option. It will cost more, and you may need to deal with building permits and other legal issues, but it may be worth it if you value your privacy or have a large family already living with you. In some locations, you can even build a small, freestanding structure or "mother-in-law house" in your backyard. If you're handy with tools, it is a way to hire yourself for a money-making project.

Randy converted his first house at age twenty three. It was a twenty-one-hundred-square-foot, two-story home. He needed help paying the mortgage, so he converted the bottom half of the house into a rental and lived upstairs. The units were completely blocked off from each other and had separate entrances. He was lucky because the house was designed with a bathroom and bedrooms on both levels. It was an easy conversion. He only had to put in a small kitchenette. The house was easily converted back to its original state as a single-family home when he sold it. We considered doing something similar with our present home, but opted to become a multi-generational household instead when Jane's mother moved in with us.

Rent out your spare bedroom for the night

There is an online service that connects travelers with people who have rooms to rent. If you have a spare bedroom, you can rent it out for $50 per night or more in some cases. You can earn more if you live in a great location and have luxury amenities. If travelers stay for multiple nights, you can really earn some extra cash from your money-making asset—your house. If you are living in an apartment, you may still be able to use the service and earn money with a spare bedroom in your apartment. The website is https://airbnb.com. There may be some concern about renting your room out to strangers. Airbnb.com has a section about safety on their website. A new on-line service, TrustCloud.com, is in beta testing and should improve the experiences of the 'sharing economy' by offering identity verification and background checks.

Rent out your whole house for a year while you travel

Want to travel but feel like you can't afford to? Put your valuables in storage or leave them with family and rent out your whole house with a year's lease. You can also leave your furniture and rent out your house fully furnished. From our limited personal experience as landlords, if your mortgage is paid in full, you can spend up to 65 percent of your rent receipts for your traveling costs. The other 35 percent of your rent receipts are for taxes, insurance, and maintenance. You may also need to spend 10 percent of your rental income for professional management to watch over the place while you are gone. These percentages can vary depending on where you live. You can save the management fee if you can get a friend or family member to watch over your house. Don't forget to call your insurance agent and get a business policy to replace your standard homeowner's insurance. Also, keep in mind that according to IRS guidelines, you need to have lived in your house for at least two out of the five years immediately preceding the sale of your house in order to keep your tax-free status when you do sell. You may be able to exclude from income any gain on the sale of your home up to a limit of $500,000 if you are married or $250,000 if you are single. That means you can travel for up to three years before coming home without worrying about your tax benefit if you decide to sell the house.

Reverse mortgages: get cash for staying in your house

If you still want to live in your home and the mortgage is fully or nearly paid off, you can stay for as long as you want and receive cash from a reverse mortgage. Your credit score does not factor in to securing the loan, and you don't have to make payments to pay your reverse mortgage back. The loan is paid in full when you pass away and the house is sold. Any equity left over after paying the reverse mortgage off goes to your estate. You are required to pay the loan in full or sell the house if you vacate your home for more than twelve months, such as if you move to a nursing home. If your kids still want to keep the house after you die or move to a nursing home, they can simply pay off the loan instead of selling the house. If the bank sells the house and there is not enough money to pay the loan, then the bank takes the loss. The bank can't come after your other assets or your children's assets.

Each homeowner must be at least age sixty-two years old to apply for the loan. If married, it is best that both spouses have their names on the loan. If only one name is on the loan and that person passes away, the surviving spouse would have to move out of the house. The home must be owned free and clear, or the existing mortgage must be paid off with the proceeds from the reverse mortgage. You must continue to pay property taxes, homeowner's insurance, and maintenance.

Your home's value, based on an appraisal, and your life expectancy determines the amount of the loan. The older you are, the larger the check will be. Interest rates and limits imposed by the government will also affect the amount you will receive. There is a mortgage limit on expensive homes if the loan is insured by the Federal Housing Authority, or FHA. That limit is $625,500.

You can accept your money in five different ways: all at once as a lump sum; equal monthly payments for as long as you live in the house; equal monthly payments for a set number of years, such as ten years; keeping a line of credit and only using money when you need it until you run out of the money provided by the loan; or any combination of the above four ways.

One of the main drawbacks to taking out a reverse mortgage is the high fees associated with the loan. A way to save on reverse mortgage fees is to not take out a loan at the bank, but have one or more of your children give you monthly check(s) instead and avoid the reverse mortgage entirely. When your house is sold after you die or vacate the premises, your children are paid back their contributions plus interest. Be sure to contact an estate attorney since this action could complicate your estate plans.

Another way to save on reverse mortgage fees and minimize interest charged by the bank is to sell your house to one of your kids, cashing out the equity in your home to shore up your finances, and then pay monthly rent back to your child for as long as you want to live in the home. The child gets rental income and can take deductions for real estate taxes, depreciation, and maintenance on their income tax filing. Once you no longer reside in the house, your child can sell the property or keep it as an investment. Conventional mortgage costs are significantly lower than the costs for a reverse mortgage in most cases.

Another downside to a reverse mortgage is that you must have enough income to maintain the house and pay the taxes and insurance, which increase each year. Otherwise, you can be in default on the reverse mortgage, and the bank can kick you out. This is something to think carefully about if you are considering this option. However, a reverse mortgage is still a good deal for those folks who do not want to move but need the money. The US Department of Housing and Urban Development (HUD) provides a list of reverse mortgage counselors who can help you determine if this option is right for you. Go to http://www.hud.gov/offices/hsg/sfh/hcc/hcs. cfm and click on your state. A new window will open. Select "Click here to narrow your search" in the left-hand corner of the page. This will take you to some dropdown boxes. In the "Counseling Service" box, one of the dropdown options is "Reverse Mortgage Counseling." Select this, and then click "Search" at the bottom of the page, which will take you to results of all of the HUD-approved reverse mortgage counseling services in your state.

Downsizing might be the way to go

If you own a big house that used to hold three kids, two dogs, and a couple of SUVs, you could sell the house and put the equity into the bank instead. If you invest the proceeds in stocks and bonds, your rate of return should be at least 5.3 percent. You could put some of the cash into a smaller house or rent an apartment. You can even try some of the other crazy ideas in this chapter, like moving in with a group of people or building a tiny house. Downsizing is a quick way to add equity to your nest egg.

Move to another location

You may find that the area where you are currently living is too darn expensive for retirement. The rent is too high, and the houses cost more than what you can afford. LA or New York, for example, are not the kind of locations that can easily support a low-cash life. If you move to a rural area or small town, such as in the Midwest or the South, you will be able to find rentals that cost very little. If you are still in a position to buy real estate, purchasing a house in a more rural area is cheaper as well, especially if you include the cost of insurance, utilities, and taxes. The cost of moving can be minimized if you decide to get rid of most of your stuff and travel light. Another bonus: a new location can bring changes to your life that can energize you. However, one possible drawback is leaving your support network of family and friends. Technology such as FaceTime and Skype can offset the distance, providing face-to-face conversations with friends and family, but building a new support network after you move is very important for your mental and physical health. How do you build such a network? Try some or all of the following:

- Join a church, synagogue, temple, or mosque, and get involved with some of the group activities.
- Take a class at your local community college.
- Work out at a gym.

- Get out with your pet at a dog park.
- Volunteer with local charity organizations.
- Search the Internet for a club or group that interests you.
- Check out book clubs that meet at your local library.

Instead of moving across the country, how about moving *out* of the country? This may offer you the opportunity to live well for even less money. You can still access your Social Security benefits from a foreign country, and even if they are your only source of income, you can live like a rich person in some places. For example, the cost of living in Belize is much lower than the cost of living in most of the United States. You can live near the ocean with tropical breezes and a laid-back lifestyle. Plus, no more shoveling snow! To find more information on living abroad, go to http://internationalliving.com. Some concerns about living outside the United States may be medical costs since Medicare will not cover you if you live out of the country, and the high crime rate of some countries. Traveling to visit family will also be more expensive.

Think tiny

A tiny house—think less than five hundred square feet—may be the best option for you. Why tiny? It is a way of life that is starting to catch on across the nation. You learn to live with much less stuff. Anything you bring with you into the tiny house is deliberately thought out. You learn what is important in your life. And since most tiny houses are on wheels, you have the freedom to move anywhere you want at a moment's notice.

These houses are built out of wood and generally sleep one to two people. Check out http://www.tumbleweedhouses.com, where you can find pictures and house plans that might suit your taste. The Tumbleweed Tiny House Company's houses on wheels range from 117 square feet to 172 square feet not counting the sleeping loft. The company can build you a custom-made home, or you can buy the plans and build your own for half the cost. The houses have a bathroom, a kitchen, and a sleeping loft. There is even space for a dining table. It is like living on a boat, and you need a different mind-set to adjust to storing supplies and living in a tight space. Again, you will need to travel light. Just think—instead of using a down payment to buy a big house and rack up debt with a mortgage, you can pay for your tiny house in full. Parking in somebody's yard, hooked up to utilities like water and electric, is legal in most areas. Maybe you can take turns visiting each one of your family and friends and pay no parking fees. You can accomplish the same by buying a small RV, which is even cheaper if it's used. You can also learn more about this trend by watching *Tiny House Nation* on FYI, which is an A&E Networks channel, or by checking out http://www.thetinylife.com.

The price of a down payment on most normal-sized houses will pay for a tiny house in full. No house payments! A tiny house also costs less to heat and cool. Taxes and insurance are less. If you adopt the minimalist lifestyle with a tiny house, you can survive on much less money, or if you have another source of income, you can accumulate a bigger nest egg.

Some of the same benefits can still be achieved with something a little larger, like a house between five hundred and eight hundred square feet, for example, if you feel claustrophobic in a tiny house or don't want to climb a loft ladder. A medium-sized house is still much more economical than the typical large house many empty nesters have today.

How about HUD?

For the truly poor retiree, one option might be the HUD housing program, which can provide seniors rent assistance with housing vouchers. The program can also help you gain access to public housing and multifamily subsidized housing that is privately owned but is subsidized by HUD. The waiting list can be as long as two to five years to obtain your living quarters, so you must plan ahead and find another option while you wait. The benefits are based on a percentage of the median income in the area where you live. For example, the average yearly income to qualify for multifamily subsidized housing is about $10,000. If you earn the average Social Security benefit amount of $15,528, you may not be able to qualify. However, there are some HUD programs that may allow higher median incomes, especially if your area has a high income level. If this option appeals to you then begin your search with http://www.hud.gov/offices/hsg/sfh/hcc/hsc.cfm. You can find a HUD-sponsored housing counseling agency for your state. The counselors there will give you advice on how to proceed.

Free—or almost free—housing

The following sections are about ways to obtain free—or almost free—housing. Some are unusual methods, but they do work. You can combine these methods with any other methods we have already covered. For example, you can rent out your whole house, move across the country, and take a job as a leasing agent of an apartment complex that offers a free apartment in return. The cash from your house being rented out can supplement your retirement income. You can always move back into your house whenever you want. If you do not own a house, then the following free housing might be just the ticket. Some of these ideas do involve working, but they come with the bonus of free rent.

Maybe you can go back home

You can move in with your kids on a temporary basis if they will have you. If you are younger, moving back home with your parents might be the way to go. Perhaps you could also stay with a brother, a sister, or a long-lost cousin for a while—at least long enough to stabilize your finances. Again, you will most likely need to travel light.

We know of a lady in her seventies who found herself without any financial support after her husband's death. The couple had owned a small business, but after taxes and debts were satisfied, there was nothing left for her retirement. Luckily, she had a fair amount of extended family. No one had the room or inclination for her to move in permanently, so she traveled between them, spending several months in each home. Family looked forward to her visits. Being retired, she could take the time to play games and read endless stories to the children. Adults enjoyed her cooking and sewing help and evenings spent playing cards or talking. If you should find yourself in a similar situation, don't discount the value you can offer to family in exchange for room and board.

House-sitting

If you are completely without a roof over your head, perhaps you could house-sit for someone. You will most likely be able to enjoy a large home all to yourself for a short period of time. The average time frame a house sitter is required ranges from two weeks to six months, so you will need to move often. Also, you may need to take care of pets and gardens as part of the deal, so liking animals and having a green thumb would be a bonus. The rent is free, and you get to visit new places often. It is kind of like being on a permanent vacation. You can find opportunities to house-sit at http://www.housesittersamerica.com. The cost to join is thirty dollars per year. If you're leaning toward a more international presence, you can visit http://www.mindmyhouse.com/index.php, which lists opportunities abroad as well as in the United States. It costs twenty dollars per year to join. To succeed in house-sitting, you have to be trustworthy, conscientious, and flexible.

By now, you see how important it is to travel light in most of the situations we have covered. It is one of the secrets of surviving a broke retirement.

Get a job as a leasing agent or as a manager of an apartment complex

Often, you receive a free apartment as compensation when you take on a job as a manager or leasing agent. If you are good with your hands, sometimes an on-site maintenance job will also score you a free apartment. The apartment can be tax-free if the employer provides the housing for their own convenience and requires you to live there as a condition of employment, so that is a nice bonus. Also, there is no commuting cost, so there is a possibility you could do without a car. You can also get the same deal as a manager of a storage facility. Remember, you will be on call day and night. You may not have as much free time as you like. Some people don't mind this, especially if they are homebodies.

If you have an RV, you might benefit from a job at an RV park. You could live in your RV—a free place to stay—and earn a little extra cash. If you like the great outdoors, you might find a caretaker job with a state or federal park, which may also come with a free place to stay. A great website to explore such opportunities is http://www.workampingjobs.com. It is a free site to find jobs that may come with a free place to park your RV with access to utilities.

You may be able to find opportunities with a hotel chain as a manager or maintenance person. If you are not the management type or good with your hands, you could be a caregiver for a disabled or aged person in exchange for a free room. There are also domestic jobs available in exchange for a room—if you don't mind doing housework.

Renovate a house for somebody else
Again, if you are good with your hands, you might be able to live rent-free in exchange for renovating a house. Most likely, this would be a short-term assignment. Depending on how much renovating is required, it could be as long as six months. There could be additional compensation that could cover your other expenses. The best way to find a person to hire you to renovate is by advertising your services on Craigslist.org. Also, check with realtors and bankers for leads.

Are you really going to live in your car?
If your situation is really desperate, you might have to consider living in your vehicle for a while. It may not be the most comfortable or safest way to live, but it can be done. If you have no money, no job, and no roof over your head, then your vehicle might be the only option (if you still have a vehicle). Hopefully, this would only be for a short period of time until you could opt for one or more of the other housing options mentioned above.

The money you save on rent or mortgage payments can add up fast and can be used to pay down debt or help build a nest egg for retirement. It may be a way to exist when there is very little money coming in to support your housing needs.

There are many rules and guidelines for living out of a vehicle, and we recommend a good book you can buy that will show you how to do it: *How to Live in a Car, Van or RV*, by Bob Wells. You can purchase it in e-book or paperback form on Amazon.com. Wells discusses how important it is to blend into the background while living in your vehicle so nobody will hassle you for not spending money parking in RV parks. He shows you the best type of vehicle to buy and ways to fix it up to make a comfortable life. The book begins with tips for getting rid of things to free up your life. Traveling light is imperative in this situation. The book goes on to explain how to shower and stay clean, how to cook, how to stay in touch with the outside world, how to use electrical power, and much more. It also discusses how to stay comfortable when it is hot or cold outside. Wells does a good job of explaining what equipment to buy and where to buy it. His list has been tested by people like him who have lived in a vehicle full time for many years. He also reveals an ingenious way to use the bathroom that makes complete sense.

There are advantages to living out of your van. First, if you are still working at a job, you can cut down your commuting cost by living very close to your place of employment. Think of the time you could save by not sitting in a traffic jam each morning. You could move to different parts of the country to take advantage of the seasons, living up north during the summer and down south during the winter. This could be a great way to see the country if you have always wanted to travel. You could select an area to be closer to your loved ones. The biggest advantage is the amount of money you can save. You can use the money for a retirement nest egg or, if you are without a job, you can exist on very little money. For some folks, that spells freedom.

A disadvantage is that it is difficult to live out of a vehicle. It can also be uncomfortable at times during extreme weather, but there are ways to deal with the weather that Bob Wells talks about in his book. It can be dangerous if you happen to park in an unsafe part of town one night or if you get chased off by the police for violating city codes. There is also some financial investment required up front to outfit your home on wheels that may require you to stay in the vehicle long enough to see a payoff, such as cooking equipment, a frame for your bed in your van and plastic boxes for storage.

It takes a special kind of person to live like a nomad, but some people love it because it gives them a degree of freedom. Others may find the idea appalling and wouldn't be caught dead living out of a vehicle. If you're part of the latter, don't despair; the other housing options we covered previously may be more appealing to you.

Health Care: The Cost of Staying Healthy

For most people, health care is the fifth most costly component of their budget—*if* they are young and healthy. However, we placed it as the second most important part of the budget because if you do have a health problem, then you could be spending a great deal more money than the average for a healthy person. According to the US Bureau of Labor Statistics, in 2013, the average American household spent about 6 percent of its annual budget on health care. According to research sponsored by the Society of Actuaries and using data from the Health Care Cost Institute, the out-of-pocket costs for health care for the average fifty-five-year-old after retirement will be nearly a quarter of a million dollars more than the out-of-pocket costs for someone who retires at age sixty-five, provided both people live to be eighty-five. In this chapter, we explore ways to cut the actual costs of seeing doctors, taking prescriptions, and undergoing expensive medical procedures. We address the subject of health insurance in a later chapter. Hopefully, you are (and will remain) in good general health. However, you or a family member may be struggling with a health issue that is currently draining your savings. We are going to show you ways to save on your costs and maybe even get some of your prescriptions for free.

How to cut the cost of medical procedures

You have to be bold. You need to ask for discounts from your doctors and medical facilities. In many cases, it works, especially if you're broke. You can negotiate a lower price, but first you need to know the fair price. You may find http://www.healthcarebluebook.com useful. The site is easy to navigate and allows you to locate certain procedures and their going "fair rate." By entering your zip code, you'll get customized results for your area. You may find that you are already getting a fair price, but most of the time, the prices quoted by your doctor or hospital are outrageous. Doctors and hospitals start with a higher list price because they know that insurance companies will negotiate for a lower price. You can compare prices and act on the one that you feel is the best. Keep in mind your insurance company may have an agreement with some providers, and that can save you money if you stay in their network. If you seek care outside of your network, your insurance company may not pay for your procedures or may pay less of the cost. Always check with your insurance company before booking a procedure.

If you need a test or other expensive procedure, ask your doctor to refer you to the lowest cost provider. Many doctors know and can share this information with you. Another way to find out is to ask your doctor or his or her staff for the Current Procedural Terminology (CPT) code of the procedure. The CPT code is the standard code all hospitals use to identify each medical procedure. Call all of your local medical facilities and ask for the billing department. Many will readily disclose the cost. Some hospitals may not release the information, but it is worth a shot. You can also use the opportunity to negotiate ahead of time for the best price. Ask if there is a sliding scale for fees, and see if the facility offers a payment plan.

Another option for some operations is to use an outpatient surgery center instead of a major hospital. Ask your doctor for a referral. You can save quite a bit of money.

For minor emergencies that are not life threatening, use an urgent care center. You can save up to 90 percent of the cost. You can find urgent care centers in your area by searching for "urgent care Kansas City," for example. Several pharmacies have also joined the health care provider game. For example, many CVS pharmacies have a Minute Clinic, and many Walgreens pharmacies have a Take Care Clinic, both of which offer urgent care. To give you an idea of savings, it may cost $950 for a visit to the ER but only $33 to $50 for the same treatment at an urgent care center. If you are experiencing a life-threatening condition, such as a heart attack, then by all means, call 911 or have someone drive you to the nearest emergency room. The urgent care center will not be able to help you. The CVS website lists symptoms that are *not* treated at their clinic:

- severe chest pain
- severe shortness of breath
- suspected poisoning
- children with temperatures of at least 104 degrees Fahrenheit
- adults with temperatures of at least 103 degrees Fahrenheit
- conditions that require practitioners to prescribe controlled substances

You can also call your local hospital's "ask a nurse" program with questions to help you gauge the severity of your condition and determine the best course of action. Many health insurance companies also offer a toll-free number for such questions. You can check the back of your insurance card to find the number to call.

Looking outside the United States for some medical procedures can also save you money. According to the nonprofit Medical Tourism Association (http://www.medicaltourismassociation.com/en/index.html), going abroad can save you 20 to 80 percent of the price you would pay in the United States for the same procedure. Medical tourism, or traveling abroad for medical care, is not new. People have been traveling to healing spas and "magical springs" for centuries. What *are* new are the reasons for such travel. Patients are now electing to have procedures done out of the country because of cost savings as well as because of procedures that are unavailable or of poor quality in their home country. Patients Beyond Borders (http://www.patientsbeyondborders.com) lists the top specialties for medical travelers as cosmetic surgery, dentistry, cardiovascular, orthopedics, cancer, reproductive, weight loss, scans, tests, health screenings, and second opinions. The organization cites Costa Rica, India, Israel, Malaysia, Singapore, South Korea, Taiwan, Thailand, Turkey, and the United States as the most popular destinations. The site also lists the average savings range for the most traveled destinations and offers an opportunity to request by e-mail a free detailed comparative cost data report by country and procedure. A liver transplant performed in the United States can cost $300,000, but the same procedure done in Taiwan might only cost $91,000. In 2008, *The Wall Street Journal* reported that Hannaford Brothers, a supermarket chain based in Maine, would cover all expenses, including travel, for employees to receive hip or knee replacement in Singapore. The Centers for Disease Control and Prevention (CDC) estimates that seven hundred fifty thousand US residents travel abroad for care each year. You can check out what the CDC says about this trend at http://www.cdc.gov/features/medicaltourism. The organization offers information about risks as well as information about how to plan to travel to another country for medical care.

Today, more than four hundred health care organizations in thirty-nine countries are accredited by the International Division of the Joint Commission, which is the organization that accredits medical facilities in the United States. Accreditation Canada and the United Kingdom Accreditation Forum are also involved with making sure facilities abroad meet the same standards as facilities in their countries. In spite of this, there are risks involved with traveling abroad to obtain medical care, and depending on your situation, these may negate the cost savings. Another source, http://www.medicaltourism.com/en/medical-tourism-guide.html, offers comprehensive definitions and links to information on topics from what to expect to why medical care is cheaper outside the Unites States, Canada, and the United Kingdom. An Internet search for medical tourism, health travel, medical travel, or global health care will deliver a large volume of information; however, we caution you to consider the source before believing everything you read. Some only want to separate you from your money without providing any real benefit.

One final note on medical travel: while many insurance companies are now on board with outsourcing medical care to other countries, currently, Medicare does not cover treatments abroad. If you are considering saving money on a procedure by going out of the country, check with your insurance provider to see what is covered.

When you receive your final medical bill, check for errors. According to the Medical Billing Advocates of America, about eight out of ten medical bills contain errors. The organization's website, http://www.billadvocates.com, provides education about medical bills and even offers specialists who will comb through your bill on your behalf and fix the errors for a small fee. It may be well worth the cost. You can also find a medical claims expert located in one of seventeen states at http://www.claims.org./refer.php. These claims professionals provide assistance to clients across the country for a fee. The website lists the available services, which range from challenging medical bills to helping negotiate providers' fees.

Lower the cost of your prescription medicine

If you don't have health insurance that pays for prescription drugs, you may qualify for assistance. There is an organization that acts as a clearinghouse to connect you with companies and programs that will provide you with low-cost or free prescriptions. The organization is called the Partnership for Prescription Assistance (PPA), and it offers services at no cost to you. The website is http://www.pparx.org/en. You can get help with 2,500 medicines through 475 patient assistance programs. Take care, though, to make sure you are accessing their site through *www.pparx.org* to ensure that you are actually dealing with PPA because there are a number of companies that misrepresent themselves as PPA and may charge you a fee or, worse, commit fraud by representing themselves as PPA to gain access to your private personal information.

Some pills can be split in half. For example, say you take a twenty-milligram pill every day, which costs $100 for a thirty-day supply. Instead, ask your doctor if he or she will prescribe a forty-milligram pill that costs $150 per month. When you split the pill in half, the thirty-day supply costs $75 instead of $100, which is a savings of $300 per year. Imagine, if you have to take four prescriptions and they all can be split, you could be looking at a total savings for the year of $1,200. Keep in mind that some medications are not meant to split—in fact, some can be downright dangerous—so ask your doctor first. You can buy a pill splitter at your local pharmacy.

Ask your doctor if he or she can prescribe a generic medication instead of a name-brand formula. You can save up to 80 percent with generic meds. Walmart has a four-dollar generic drug plan in forty-nine states. Target has announced a similar plan. There can be up to three hundred generic drugs at the four-dollar level.

Buying from conglomerates like Target or Walmart generally saves you money on prescriptions. You can also buy cheaper if you buy your prescriptions in rural areas instead of city centers.

Your doctor may be able to tell you if there is another drug that was used commonly to treat your affliction in the past but has been replaced by a newer class of drug. The older therapy may work just as well but will cost much less.

You can also ask your doctor for samples. He or she might have your drug in the office and can give it to you for free.

See if your health insurance company offers a mail-order option. You save money by ordering a three-month supply through the mail. You may get the same benefit by asking your local pharmacist if he or she can give you a three-month supply for a reduced price. This is not the same as ordering your prescriptions over the Internet from another country. When you do that, you risk not receiving the pill you need. It can be fake or can contain ingredients that may be dangerous.

Buy used home medical devices

Items such as scooters, power chairs, walkers, and a variety of daily living aids can be purchased used. As we age, the odds are that most of us will at some point need a little assistance with something. The website http://www.usedhme.com offers free listings of used home medical equipment for sale in your area. It's similar to eBay, and it's simple to use because it lists only home medical equipment. If you find yourself needing to purchase medical equipment, check this site out first. You may be able to save a significant amount of money.

Dental

The best way to save money on dental care is to focus on preventative care. Stopping cavities before they start costs very little compared with fixing them. Having at least two dental checkups per year will help you stay on top of the situation. Having your teeth cleaned during your checkups is preventative and will be paid by your dental insurance if you have it.

Finding low-cost dental insurance can save you approximately 75 percent of your dental costs. Say dental insurance for you and your spouse costs $411 per year. If your dentist charges $140 per cleaning, and you both have two cleanings each year as recommended, that adds up to $560 per year. Most dental insurance pays 100 percent of the cost for such cleanings, so having insurance can actually save you money. Paying for the dental insurance is cheaper than paying for the cleaning visits out of pocket. More important, it saves on more expensive dental care in the future by preventing major problems. Fixing a small cavity discovered during your biannual cleaning is significantly less expensive than undergoing a root canal.

Prevention magazine tells us good dental care is not just about healthy teeth; it is also about your total health as well. Bad teeth may increase risk for other health problems, such as heart disease and diabetes to name a few, which can increase your healthcare costs.

While Medicaid does cover some dental care, Medicare does not, so it is important to find dental insurance you can afford. One source for affordable dental insurance is http://www.ehealthinsurance.com/dental-insurance, where you can search for dental insurance in your area and compare several different plans.

There are a few other tips for affordable or even free dental care. The National Oral Health Information Clearing House at http://www.nidcr.nih.gov/OralHealth/PopularPublications/FindingLowCostDentalCare/ provides information about dental schools, clinical trials, and other sources of low-cost dental care. You can call your state dental society or association to find out if there is a dental or dental hygiene school in your area. Often, dental care is available on a sliding scale based on income—or can even be free—if offered by students under the close supervision of certified dentists and hygienists.

America's Dentists Care Foundation Missions of Mercy operates in several states and is a source of free dental care for the underserved population in America. For more information, check out http://www.adcfmom.org. Click on "find an event" to locate a clinic event on the nationwide schedule near you.

Mail-order eyeglasses

You can easily spend $300 to upwards of $500 for eyeglasses here in the United States. You can save 90 percent if you order online. That's $450 extra to spend in your budget—$900 if your spouse wears glasses as well.

In our opinion, the best website to visit for ordering your glasses is http://www.zennioptical.com. The site is easy to navigate and has great customer service. You enter the information from the prescription your optometrist gave you on the website. Be sure to get the papillary distance measurements from your doctor so when the glasses are prepared for you, they will fit properly.

With Zenni Optical online, you can even "try on" glasses. You upload a picture of your face and click on a pair of glasses you like. The glasses will "magically" appear on your face in the picture. There are hundreds of glasses in all different colors and styles to choose from. Zenni Optical prices start at $6.95 for simple glasses with a $4.95 shipping charge. You can order progressives, lined bifocals and tinting as well as a host of other options. They ship to you in seven to fourteen business days.

Hearing aids

Noise, from the lawn mowers to rock concerts, affects your hearing, and the probability that you will suffer some hearing loss actually increases rapidly after age sixty. Some studies put the percentage of people with significant enough hearing loss to benefit from some kind of hearing assistance at 55 percent after the age of seventy-five. Prices vary according to region, but according to a recent article on AARP's website, the average cost of a midlevel hearing aid is about $4,500. You can buy hearing aids online for a couple hundred dollars, but you get what you pay for. As you can see, correcting a hearing problem is expensive. Consumer Reports offers a comprehensive guide to hearing aids (http://www.consumerreports.org/cro/hearing-aids/buying-guide.htm), from selecting a hearing aid provider and getting a thorough examination to paying for your hearing aid. The website includes links to organizations such as the Lions Club Lions Affordable Hearing Aid Project and Sertoma (short for Service to Mankind), which offer assistance to those who can't afford hearing aids. The Consumer Reports buying guide also offers tips on obtaining tax deductions for your hearing aid needs.

—⚏—

Transportation

Getting around town in your own set of wheels can eat up a large portion of your budget. In a 2013 survey, the Department of Labor found that the average household spends almost 14 percent of its budget on transportation. Transportation can be the second biggest component of your budget.

For the 2015 tax year, the IRS claims it cost the average driver fifty-seven and a half cents a mile to drive a car and allows you to deduct this cost on your taxes if it is related to your business. Some people can drive for much less by buying used cars, but driving your own car is expensive when you consider the total cost, including insurance, maintenance, gas, taxes, depreciation, and parking and toll fees. It you drive ten thousand miles a year, you could be looking at a $5,750 budget expense. But wait—it's actually more when you consider the income tax you have to pay from your wages or investments to come up with that $5,750. It can be as much as $7,700 per year with tax. Imagine what it cost you if you drive more miles. Just cutting this cost in half by following some of the ideas in this chapter can add $3,850 or more to your savings—or allow you to work less.

If you want to raise a tidy sum of cash to pay down your debts or pay for your retirement, then try to do without a car. You can still get around quite well without a car, depending on where you live. If you are in the market for a job, secure employment before deciding which apartment or house to occupy. Once you find the job, you can move into an apartment or house within walking distance of your employment, unless your previous housing situation is more profitable. Another option is to look for a place to live that is close to public transportation, such as a bus route. It is a nice perk to have nearby services such as a grocery store and a bank. Bonus: it will help you stay healthy when you have to walk every day.

Just think—if it costs fifty-seven and a half cents per mile to drive, which includes depreciation, maintenance, insurance, taxes, and gas, then a thirty-mile round trip costs $17.25. That is about two and a half hours of work at $10 per hour at a part-time job after income taxes. If you have to drive thirty miles to and from work, you are giving up almost one-fourth of your eight-hour shift just to get there. If you do drive a great distance to your job, then it better be a good-paying job to make it worthwhile. You may find in retirement that your options are limited to only low-paying, part-time work. Some make the mistake of looking only at the cost of gas to drive to work. Remember, you have to replace your car eventually if you are driving all over the place, and that will cost a lot.

If you only need a car a couple days per month because you live close to your job and groceries, you can always rent a car to drive to a doctor's appointment or to stock up on supplies from an all-day shopping trip at stores not near your home. This is still cheaper than paying for your own car. In some cities, you can even rent a car by the hour. Check out Zipcar at http://www.zipcar.com.

Uber (http://www.uber.com) and Lyft (http://www.lyft.com) are two companies that provide an app for your smartphone. They match you up with freelance drivers who use their own cars to pick you up and drive you wherever you want to go. We've heard great things about Uber and Lyft, and they can be valuable assets to you in your quest to do without a car. We checked our area, and Uber charges $35 to $45 for a fifteen-mile trip one way. If you can get by only using them for a couple of round trips a month at $140, you come out ahead when you consider how much it costs to keep your own car, which can run as much as $300 or more per month.

Maybe you need a car because you like to live in a rural area, you are exposed to harsh weather conditions, or you have a large family. Then, buy used cars instead of new. Buying a three- to five-year-old car is much cheaper because most of the depreciation cost has been paid by the first owner. Go to the library to check out Consumer Reports for the most dependable car to buy. A web search may also yield the same information with the key phrase "most dependable car." According to the National Highway Traffic Safety Administration, the average lifespan of a car before it is sold as scrap is 152,137 miles. If you can research and find a dependable car that can travel two hundred thousand miles with no major repair issues, you can save quite a bit on transportation costs.

Other tips include carpooling to your job and planning your errands. Combine five or six trips into one when shopping, visiting friends, and going to the doctor. Wait a few days, making a list until it is full, and then do your running around.

If you must have a new car, then maybe you can join the next revolution in economical transportation and buy the Elio car. We think it will be the next Volkswagen and believe you will see a lot of them on the road. These cars will be in production in the middle part of 2016. We were so impressed with the features that we put a large deposit down and are number 3,969 in line to get one.

What's so great about this car? The price, for one thing. It's only $6,800 brand new, with a three-year or thirty-six-thousand-mile warranty. And it gets eighty-four miles per gallon on the highway and forty-nine miles per gallon in the city on regular gasoline. It's not a hybrid. It uses a conventional gasoline engine, and most replacement parts can be found at your local auto parts store. The Elio comes with safety features such as three airbags, an antilock braking system, and a reinforced roll cage frame.

With the low price, lower maintenance costs, and great gas savings, the Elio will pay for itself. If you replace your old car that gets twenty-five miles per gallon, the money you save on gas over ten years at ten thousand miles per year will pay for the Elio. Just think, a brand-new car for free. You can't get any cheaper than that! You can check out Elio's website at http://www.eliomotors.com. The car holds two people in cockpit style with one person up front and one in the back. It has two wheels up front and one wheel in back. It is completely enclosed and has heating and air conditioning, power locks and windows, and an AM/FM stereo.

The Elio is built as a commuter car since most people drive to work alone. You may still need a large car as your primary vehicle if you have kids at home or need to haul a lot of stuff around town. However, if there are only one or two people in your household, then the Elio would be a very cheap way to get around and could be your only car—essentially for free.

—m—

Food

Food is the third most expensive component of the average budget. According to a 2013 Department of Labor survey, the average household spends almost 10 percent of its budget on food. In addition, the average household spends about 40 percent of its food cost on eating out—an expensive option for feeding yourself.

When money is tight and you need to spend the least amount on food, what are the best items to stock your pantry? To stretch your food budget, buy less processed food. Instead, buy raw ingredients in bulk and process them yourself. You can buy flour, oil, and yeast to make your own bread and pizzas. Buy dry beans and rice. Buy eggs for the cheapest protein, and buy oatmeal for your breakfast. Speaking of protein, the less meat you buy and the closer you stay to a vegetarian diet, the more money you will save. Some studies claim that a vegetarian diet is also healthier. Peanut butter goes a long way when making sandwiches and cookies. Pasta is filling and tasty. Buying cheese in big blocks is a good source of protein and makes a great snack. To eat healthy, try adding colorful vegetables to your meals. Produce can be expensive, but a little goes a long way, and sometimes you can even grow your own. Potatoes in five-pound bags are inexpensive and make great casseroles or simple side dishes. For a fruit snack, buying bananas is the cheapest at about twenty-five cents per banana in most places. Buying with coupons is not always the best way to save money since you will be buying high-priced processed foods with the coupon savings built into the price of the product. Just buying off-brand items is usually cheaper than buying national brands with coupons. Cut out soda; it is too expensive and not healthy for you. Instead, drink lemon water or tea (hot or iced).

Discount grocers, such as Aldi, and day-old bread stores offer good food at reasonable prices. Your local farmers' market may have great bargains at the end of the day when farmers don't want to take home unsold produce.

Make your own frozen dinners. Take a Saturday afternoon to cook several meals ahead of time and pop them in your freezer. They will be ready to microwave when you don't have time to prepare a meal from scratch. Buying frozen meals from the grocery store, however, will wreck your food budget.

Eating out is fun but very expensive. If you have a partner, you can split a meal while dining out. It saves on calories and cash. Drinking only water and skipping the dessert will make dining out that much more affordable. Only eating out once in a while makes it a special occasion. Limit yourself to two nights out per month. For other nights that you want to entertain, have a potluck at your house or a friend's house. Have everyone bring a dish or dessert. You still get to hang out with friends or family but at a fraction of the cost of eating out. It can be more fun as well.

Food stamps might be available if your finances are really in bad shape. You can contact your local government agency to apply for assistance. An Internet search for "how do I access food stamps in xxx" (xxx is your state) will return information on the program, including how to apply.

If food stamps don't provide enough food or you don't qualify for them, you can contact your local food pantries. Some churches will also have food available at no or low cost. Great sources of information about food pantries in your area include http://www.foodpantries.org, http://www.feedingamerica.org, and http://www.ampleharvest.org/find-pantry.php.

―∭―

Insurance

We have a friend who doesn't believe in insuring anything, even his house. State regulations are the only reason he has car insurance. He's only one bad storm away from financial disaster because he doesn't have the savings needed to make major repairs to his home if necessary. While we're all for finding creative ways to cut insurance costs, we don't recommend ignoring insurance altogether; it's a valuable tool to protect your assets, whatever they may be.

According to a 2013 survey by the US Department of Labor, personal insurance and pensions make up the fourth most expensive component for most household budgets. In fact, the average household spends $5,528 per year, or almost 9 percent of its budget, on insurance. If you can find a way to cut insurance costs, it can go a long way toward fixing your retirement.

What's the most effective way of cutting insurance costs? By drastically changing your lifestyle, you will find savings automatically. If you have been living a conventional life, you may have to pay for insurance on a four-bedroom house, two cars, a couple of life insurance policies, and possibly a disability insurance policy. This could cost upwards of $5,000 per year. You can cut this cost to almost zero. How?

Change your lifestyle to a point to which the insurance is not required. For example, when you sell your house and downsize to an apartment or become a tenant in somebody else's home, you eliminate the need for homeowner's insurance. You may want to consider renter's insurance, but it's a fraction of the cost of homeowner's insurance. You can set your life up to reduce your transportation needs, such as by moving closer to the places you need to go. You can walk and use public transportation—and sell both of the cars and cancel the car insurance. If the kids have moved out and you feel that your spouse can survive without you if you die, then you may not find it important to keep paying for life insurance. Life insurance can be eliminated in many instances; however, keep in mind that whole life insurance policies actually have cash value that can be useful. For example, you can take a loan out against your policy, or cancel the policy to get the cash out. Of course, if you want to leave an estate to your kids or a charity, you may want to keep the life insurance. If you are retired and no longer working at a job for which your disability insurance was covering you, then there is no need for this insurance, either.

As you can see, if you really are in a dire situation with your finances, then making tough choices about your lifestyle can make a big impact on this part of your budget. You may need to let go of the life that you are used to and embrace a new way of living. It can be exciting when, for example, you are interacting with new roommates who become your friends. Roommates could be your existing friends, but they could also be new friends that you never would have had if you hadn't made the decision to sell your house and share the cost of housing. You might lose twenty pounds and get back in shape because you decide to get rid of your car and walk all over the neighborhood for most of your shopping needs. You might decide that your grown kids can take care of themselves, so you no longer have a need to leave them with a large estate financed by insurance. The talk you have with your kids about your finances may bring you closer together, and all family members may realize that living in the moment, spending time with loved ones, and not taking each other for granted is more important than an inheritance.

Whoa. *Slow down*, you say. *I'm not ready to make such drastic changes to my life.* Maybe your finances are not that bad and you still have a need for most of the insurance that we tried to eliminate. If so, there are steps to reduce the cost of insurance without getting rid of it altogether.

First, if you can increase your deductible for your house, health, and car insurance, then you can cut your premiums by quite a bit. Be sure you have enough savings to cover the amount of your deductible.

Second, paying your premiums in one lump sum per year, instead of paying monthly, can save some money.

Third, keep your credit score high. If your credit score is quite a bit above the national average of 689, then your insurance premiums will be lower in most states. You can save hundreds every year on insurance just by being financially responsible.

Fourth, if you do decide to move to another area of the country, be sure to check out the insurance rates ahead of time. You may be shocked to find much higher insurance rates in certain parts of the country. If you do it right, you may find an area to live that may actually lower your insurance premiums.

Fifth, if you have riders on your homeowner's policy to cover that antique brooch your great-aunt gave you, for example, save on the cost by placing the brooch in a safe deposit box, eliminating the need for the rider. Another example: if you belong to AAA and your towing costs are covered, then you might not need a rider on your auto insurance for the same coverage. Check to see which option is more affordable.

Don't overlook the smaller savings that can add up, such as discounts for taking safe driver classes or putting all of your necessary insurance with the same company. Many insurance companies offer a discount for covering home and auto together, for example. We were surprised by some of the discounts we discovered at Bankrate.com, which provides free rate information and advice on a large range of financial products, including insurance. You can explore the site to compare companies, prices, and products and to find out what discounts are available.

Health insurance is a big subject. If you are in the market for health insurance, then investigate the Affordable Care Act website for your state or visit healthcare.gov. You can also find information at http://www.einsurance.com. Again, having a large deductible can save you money if you're relatively healthy, but be sure you have enough savings to cover your deductible.

Once you are over the age of sixty-five, there is a 40 percent chance that you will need nursing home care. According to the 2014 Genworth Cost of Care Survey, the median annual cost for a nursing home in the United States is $77,380 for a semiprivate room and $87,600 for a private room. According to the government's latest National Nursing Home Survey, the average stay in a nursing home is 835 days, or about two years and three months. Thus, you can see that nursing home care will cost quite a bit. Long-term care insurance is desirable but very expensive and, depending on your overall health, can be difficult to get. The average premium is almost $2,000 per year for a fifty-five-year-old man, according to the American Association for Long-Term Care Insurance. If your net worth is less than $200,000 when you begin your retirement, then you are better off without long-term care insurance because you most likely have spent so much of your nest egg that you can rely on Medicaid for nursing home care by the time you need it

If you're able, you can save up to half the amount of nursing home costs by moving to an assisted living apartment. Sometimes having in-home care can be as much as 40 percent cheaper than living in a nursing home. However, depending on what medical needs you have, in-home care can be even more expensive than a nursing home. Another option is to sell your house, if it is paid in full, to pay for the nursing home care. If you still have a spouse living in the home, then a reverse mortgage may be an option.

As you can see, insurance can take up a large portion of your income, but it doesn't have to. By making simple changes to your lifestyle, you can reduce the cost of the insurance protection you need.

—ᴍ—

Taxes

Taxes are often an overlooked budget item. There are many ways to reduce the amount paid to Uncle Sam. We will not go into the details of all the deductions you can claim as a taxpayer, but you can easily find out at http://www.irs.gov. You can also check out such books from the library as J. K. Lasser's *Your Income Tax* series. This guide is an excellent reference; a new book comes out each year.

Reducing your living expenses can also reduce your taxes, which helps in the process of reaching your goals. For example, if your goal is to cut $20,000 from your budget, a lot of the heavy lifting will be achieved by the tax savings, which can be up to 20 percent or more. When you cut $16,000 from your living expenses, such as housing and transportation, an additional $4,000 will be saved on taxes you would have paid if you had withdrawn the full $20,000 from a taxable retirement account or if you had gone to work to earn the $20,000. Of course, this depends on your state and city tax rates.

Retirees are likely to have more health issues than the general population because of their age, and they can benefit from the deduction for the miles driven to and from their medical procedures. Taking deductions for mileage is often overlooked, and retirees may have quite a few miles to claim. For the 2015 tax year, the deduction is twenty-three cents per mile.

Retirees are also more likely to volunteer their time to charity organizations since they have more time on their hands. You can claim fourteen cents per mile for this activity for the 2015 tax year.

There is a profitable tax strategy that can be summed up in one word: timing. The timing of certain actions can substantially reduce your taxes. For example, if you are able to pay two years' worth of real estate taxes to your county during one year, and claim those real estate taxes on the

Schedule A of your federal tax return, you may go over the standard deduction amount easily, which will save you taxes. The standard deduction is what you can claim if you don't itemize on Schedule A. The standard deduction for tax year 2015 is $12,600 for a married couple and $6,300 for single taxpayers.

When withdrawing money from a traditional IRA to add to your other income, the total income is taxable if it is more than the deductions you can claim on your tax return. If you find yourself with less income than your deductions, then take out extra money from your IRA to equal your deductions. It's tax-free up to that point. If you don't need the money, just put it into a savings account for the following year. This also works if you have one-time major losses, such as the ones we cover in the next paragraph. Take out enough income from your IRA to equal the losses.

Another timing situation to consider is when would be the best time to convert your traditional IRA to a Roth IRA. When you do this, you pay tax on the amount you convert at the effective tax rate you have at the time you convert the funds. However, if you have large losses to offset the amount of your transfer, then you time the IRA transfer to occur in the same year as your losses. Such losses include nonbusiness theft or a catastrophe such as a house fire, earthquake, or hurricane. If the insurance didn't cover the full amount, it can be claimed on your Schedule A for a deduction. You must subtract one hundred dollars and 10 percent of your adjusted gross income for the year from your loss to determine the amount of the deduction.

You may also have had a major medical procedure and expenses that your health insurance didn't cover, which will offset the Roth IRA conversion. If you have enough losses, your Roth conversion could be tax-free. There is an incentive to transfer your traditional IRA funds to a Roth IRA because your withdrawals in the future will be tax-free. Another situation you avoid with a Roth IRA is the government requirement that you start withdrawing funds from your traditional IRA when you turn seventy and a half. You may want to leave the funds in your Roth retirement accounts compounding tax-free well into your eighties instead of paying taxes starting at age seventy and a half on the required withdrawals from a traditional IRA.

Finally, there is a way to time the withdrawals from your IRA to avoid paying the 10 percent penalty if you are under the age of fifty-nine and a half. It is called the 72(t) election, and this procedure is explained in the Appendix in the back of this book. If you fall into a situation in which you need to access funds tied up in an IRA and may be subject to this penalty, the 72(t) election can help.

—〰—

Debt

If you still have debt, this section is where we show you how to find ways to pay it down. The first important step is to create a budget. We have to live within our means. Living on less than you earn will generate an excess cash flow that can be used to pay down your debt. With a budget, you will know ahead of time how much you have coming in as income and how much is going out as expenses. If you spend more than you earn, then you will be adding more debt, and you will never get your loans paid off.

If you don't know how much money will be coming into your life in the coming year, then just make an effort to guess. Budgets are not exact. Budgeting is mostly a guessing game as to what will happen in the future, but you must start somewhere, and estimating what will happen may still help you. If you can't cut your expenses to less than your income, then it's time to find ways to earn income, and we cover that in Part III of this book.

Step two is to pay off the debt with the highest interest rate first and work your way down your list of loans. Include your credit card balances. Pay the minimum balance on all of your loans except for the one with the highest interest rate. On that one, pay more than the minimum balance. Try to double or triple the payment amount, and continue this strategy until the amount is paid in full.

By following the budget-cutting methods in this book, you should be able to find the extra cash to add to your loan payment. Once the most expensive loan is paid off, use the money you have been putting toward that loan and add to the minimum payment you were making on the loan with the second highest rate. Once this second loan is paid, add that payment amount to the minimum payment of the third loan; continue until it is all paid.

Once all of your loans are paid, reward yourself with a special treat bought with cash equal to the last payment you made. Then, make a promise to yourself that from now on, you will pay with cash and not credit.

If you find it more convenient to use credit cards than cash, you can keep one credit card and pay it in full each month. Try to find a credit card that has cash-back rewards. The cash rewards you accumulate will add to your income. The important thing is to avoid carrying credit card balances month to month, which accumulates interest fees.

The third step is to take advantage of an offer such as 0 percent or a low interest rate on balances transferred to another credit card. Use this method to move debt off higher-interest cards. Keep in mind that balance transfer fees are often 3 to 5 percent—something to think about when considering this option. If you think you can pay off your cards in a short amount of time, there is no need to transfer the balance and pay the extra fees.

Some people use the equity in their home to pay down credit cards with second mortgages and line of credit loans. We don't suggest this method because it may be an expensive loan with the closing costs. You will be better off reducing your expenses and using the free cash flow to pay down your debts fast. Skip the house mortgage.

If you have a whole life insurance policy from which you can borrow money at a lower rate than what you are paying on your credit cards, then you can come out ahead. It is another method of transferring the higher-rate loan to a lower-rate loan. If you no longer have a need for the life insurance policy, then cancel your policy and use the cash value that you built up over the years toward paying down your loans.

The fourth step is to sell unnecessary household goods or expensive toys, such as boats, motorcycles, jet skis, and collectibles. You can sell on Craigslist or eBay or hold rummage sales to generate a sizable amount of cash that may pay most—if not all—of your loans.

Finally, you may find yourself with so much debt over your head that bankruptcy may be the only option. Bankruptcy is beyond the scope of this book. You should contact a bankruptcy lawyer for professional advice if you are considering this route.

What we will say is that bankruptcy should not be taken lightly. There are consequences. A bankruptcy lowers your credit score. If you have to buy another house or find another apartment to rent, a bankruptcy, which shows up on a credit check, may prevent you from doing so, at least in a nice and safe neighborhood. If you look for a new job, potential employers may run a credit check to determine if you are employable. Also, your car and house insurance premiums may increase substantially, putting a crimp in your cash flow. The IRS may come knocking on your door if you are relieved of any debts because you may need to pay taxes on the discharged amount. You could have to pay as much as one-third of the debt to the tax man anyway after it is all said and done. You might as well just pay off the darn debt in the first place and be done with it.

Believe it or not, bankruptcy could have an effect on your love life as well. It is beginning to be a common practice around the country for single folks to ask for a credit score before they seriously start dating someone. Finally, there is the "living with yourself" factor. For some, the idea of not honoring their obligations can cause guilt and sleepless nights. If you cannot keep promises to other people, how can you expect to keep promises to yourself? However, for certain situations, such as major medical expenses beyond your control, bankruptcy may be the only option. Again, check with a bankruptcy lawyer before going this route. Keep in mind that you must receive credit counseling prior to filing bankruptcy. A credit-counseling agency educates consumers as their primary function and may also offer debt consolidation services and negotiate with creditors to reduce interest rates or waive late and over-the-limit fees. There may be costs for such services, but most reputable agencies offer sliding scale fees based on your income.

Restoring credit is a lengthy process. Some credit repair schemes involve illegal practices. Claims to restore credit quickly may be associated with fraud and identity theft. So, be careful out there. You have access to resources so you can make sure you are dealing with a reputable agency. The National Foundation for Credit Counseling (NFCC) is an independent nonprofit that accredits social service programs in the United States and Canada, including credit-counseling services. The organization ensures that such agencies use appropriate checks and balances to protect the consumer.

The following sites can help in your quest to find a credit counselor.

http://www.consumer.ftc.gov/articles/0153-choosing-credit-counselor

http://www.usa.gov/topics/money/credit/debt/out-of-control.shtml

Hopefully, you will be successful in paying off your loans, but it takes more than making an effort to pay down your debt. You have to change your habits regarding how you spend money. Keeping an eye on your budget may help you stay on the path. You also need to tame the impulsive beast within you that arises when you see something you want to buy but don't have the cash for. That will be an important part of your new lifestyle. It means counting to ten and even waiting a month or two before deciding if what you want is really important. It may mean buying what you really need—or want—secondhand from a thrift store or Craigslist.

For some, the thrill of shopping for their desired item is more fun than actually owning it. How many pairs of shoes do you really need? Just look in your closet, and you're likely to find items you bought but have hardly ever worn. If you bought something on credit, you still might be paying it off—even if it's something that you never used. Let's go back to the thrill of an impulse buy. Sometimes, instead of actually purchasing something, you might find it fun to look but stop at the point that you pull out your charge card. Just walk away. It's like shooting wild animals on safari with a camera instead of a gun. Using a credit card is like using a gun on safari, your purchases are the dead animals you bring home. Just like using a camera on safari, you can still enjoy the hunt, searching online for the right fit and color, going to the mall to window-shop, but walking away at the last minute—with no debt—after you find your prize. Take a picture of the item with your phone instead of charging it to your credit card. Add the picture to your collection. You will have no dead animals taking up space in your closets, just memories of the hunt.

Develop the discipline to walk away. You can still enjoy the hunt, which is the fun part of shopping. If this won't work for you, and you have the need to actually purchase items, consider selling your shopping skills as a buyer for those who need items purchased but don't have the time or desire to actually shop. You could turn your talent as a shopper into a part-time business. Check out http://www.taskrabbit.com for information on how to sell your services as a personal shopper.

—◊◊—

Having Fun with Entertainment, Hobbies, Traveling, and Pets

How much does it cost to have fun? If you do it right, it can cost next to nothing. There are a number of free things you can do for entertainment. For example, going for a walk with a loved one to the park doesn't cost anything. Many cities often sponsor free concerts. Check out the community calendar in the city or town where you live. Many will have a list of events you can attend for free. If you live in a city with a symphony, civic orchestra, opera, or theater group then you might be able to take in the show by attending a dress rehearsal, many of which are open to the public at little or no cost. You could also volunteer with these organizations and see all the shows you want for free. Some museums and zoos have a free day for residents living in their area.

Other things you can do for entertainment: get involved with community sports as a spectator or participant, go to a friend's house and play cards or board games (you can even have a potluck dinner at the same time to cut down on eating out), take up photography and take pictures with your digital camera or phone, learn a foreign language by tapping into podcasts for free, take up genealogy and study your ancestors using the Internet and your local library, go to a community swimming pool, take music lessons online and learn how to play an instrument, join a book club, and check out special movie deals at your local movie theater (several in our vicinity offer five-dollar movies during weekdays when there aren't normally crowds).

Hobbies can be expensive, but there are ways to cut costs. You can buy used materials for your projects or find things people want to give away for free at http://www.freecycle.org. You can support your hobby by teaching classes on it. It may be fun to share your knowledge and earn the cash to pay for your hobby. If you are prolific with your hobby and create more items than you can store around the house, selling your creations might earn some income. Some people have simple hobbies, such as reading. You don't have to spend any money on books; you can simply check out books from the library. Speaking of the library, you can entertain yourself with movies from its large collection of DVDs. It's much cheaper than paying twenty dollars for you and your friend to see a movie at the cinema.

Traveling to faraway places for the adventurous spirit can be prohibitive if you are broke, but you can still manage it with a few creative methods. You can work for your travel ticket and a place to stay. Resorts and cruise ships need people to work for them.

You can teach in a foreign country that you want to visit. It requires a college degree and certification as well as a commitment to work for a set period of time, but you will be able to explore places that would be un-attainable otherwise. We have friends who spent time teaching English in South Korea and are now teaching in China. A website for teaching abroad is http://www.ciee.org. There may be volunteer opportunities for free trav-el with the Peace Corps, which requires a commitment of twenty-seven months. You also have to work for your room and board.

As we mentioned earlier, house-sitting is a great option for free lodging around the world. You watch over a house while somebody is gone. It can be a two-week to six-month assignment. You get a free home to stay in while being able to explore some exotic locations. You may need to take care of pets and plants as part of the deal. You can join sites such as http://www.housesitters-america.com, http://caretaker.org, and http://www.mindmyhouse.com/index.php. The yearly fees range from twenty dollars to sixty dollars.

You can cut down on hotel costs by staying in someone's home for a few nights. The website http://www.airbnb.com has listings in many cities around the world. Someone may have a bedroom to rent for the night at a third of the cost of a hotel room. You can even become a member your-self and earn extra money renting out a room in your apartment or house. That's money you can use for traveling.

Another idea is a complete home swap. You have someone stay in your home while you stay in their home. The person can be halfway across the world. The websites http://www.stay4free.com for international locations and http://homelink.org for domestic locations are a good place to start. There are also http://offers.homeexchange.com/lpv03/free-trial/#from_home and http://us.intervac-homeexchange.com, which are among other sites to explore. They all charge a fee to join, but you will come out ahead, saving on hotel costs.

Pets are expensive. If you can do without Fido, you might be better off. However, for some, having a pet is a stress reliever and therapeutic. Pets become members of the family, so doing without them is nonnegotiable. Hugging a stuffed toy dog isn't the same. There's really no substitute for being greeted at the door with a wet tongue and a wagging tail.

If you are someone who needs a pet, then budget for it. According to the ASPCA (www.aspca.org), the typical yearly cost for care is $1,314 for a small dog and $1,843 for a large dog. For a cat, it costs an average of $1,035 per year. If you have more than one pet, costs can easily add up to over $5,000 per year, especially if you add the cost of paying income taxes on the earnings needed to pay for your pet's maintenance. If you are curious, the ASPCA says it costs $1,055 per year to keep a rabbit, $705 per year for a guinea pig, $270 for a small bird, and $235 for fish. You have to pay for pet food, examinations, vaccinations, and heartworm and flea/tick preventative care. Also, add in litter for cats and possible insurance coverage for high-cost emergencies.

If you love pets but find you can't afford them, there are lots of pet owners who would love to have someone watch their pets when they travel. You can earn some extra cash and indulge in some pet time. It's also attractive to the pet owners, who can avoid the high costs of kennels while knowing that their adored animal has some quality one-on-one time with a pet lover.

—⚏—

Bad Habits

Most enjoy their bad habits, but boy, can they be costly! Take cigarettes, for example. If you smoke, you pay on average $5.51 for a pack. If you live in New York, the cost is much higher at $14.50 per pack. So, if you smoke one pack a day, you are spending $2,011 per year, or up to $2,700 when you factor in paying taxes on your earnings. But wait, if you factor in the hidden costs such as direct health care costs, workplace productivity losses, and premature death, the actual cost is $18.05 per pack, or $8,800 per year with income taxes. Quitting smoking has the same effect as having a $220,000 nest egg throwing off a 4 percent distribution, which is money you don't need to accumulate if you don't smoke. The information on the cost of cigarettes was provided by the American Lung Association and reflects 2014 prices.

A report published by the New England Journal of Medicine claims that on average, smokers die ten years earlier than nonsmokers. One out of five deaths in America is attributed to smoking. That is four hundred eighty thousand deaths per year. And while you're waiting for smoking to kill you, you may be suffering from serious illnesses that are related to the deadly habit like cancer, heart disease, stroke, diabetes, or lung disease.

A study by the New England Journal of Medicine claims that smokers pay on average 40 percent more in healthcare costs than nonsmokers.

If you are a rebel and enjoy your bad habits, then enjoy. Just budget for them. If you are unable to reduce costs somewhere else in your budget to make room for your bad habits, then you will need to somehow earn extra income to pay for them.

But if you know that quitting a bad habit like smoking may make you richer and healthier, and you want to achieve that, then you can learn how to break a bad habit. We didn't cover the cost of other bad habits, such as drinking, overeating, constantly eating out, drugs, or gambling because each person indulges in their habits on different levels, but you can find out how much your bad habits are costing you by keeping track of your spending and creating a budget.

According to the CDC, if you are a smoker, you are not alone if you feel that you want to quit. The majority—68.9 percent—of adult smokers want to quit, and 42.7 percent made an attempt to quit in the past year. But how exactly can you break a bad habit?

Most experts suggest the following steps. First, you need to make a conscious decision to change your behavior. Define the habit you want to stop. Note when the undesirable behavior happens. Is there a certain time of day, a memory, or a smell that triggers the behavior? Identify what emotions you have at the time, and that will help you figure out why you do it, which will help you to stop.

It may be a good idea to carry a journal and write in it each time you get the urge to indulge in a bad habit. Your goal really isn't to stop the bad habit but instead replace it with another healthier habit—a positive habit that will come close to giving you the same payoff as the bad habit. Mostly, it's stress and boredom that cause you to cross that line. Finding a way to relieve your stress and boredom with a substitute for your old habit will work. It also helps to meditate and visualize succeeding.

There is power in numbers. Find someone else trying to do the same thing you are doing, such as trying to stop overeating. You can hold each other accountable and give one another encouragement. Joining groups such as Alcoholics Anonymous or Weight Watchers can also be helpful.

It helps to admit that you have a problem and then deal with it. Changing your environment may work if pure willpower does not. If you find that you smoke if you are in a bar, then stay out of bars and share a drink or two with friends at your house.

It may take up to twenty-one days to change your habit. A very important thing to remember is that most of us who try to quit a bad habit will slip. Don't kick yourself, and don't give up. Just get back on the horse and try it again. It's not black and white. It may be messy with occasional relapses, but the only way to fail is to not try.

If you make a goal and achieve it, then reward yourself with something nice. The reward is positive reinforcement and gives you something tangible to work toward.

Finally, seek professional mental help if you are dealing with strong emotional problems or depression related to your habit. You may need treatment that is beyond just trying to change a habit. The small investment in professional help will yield a larger payoff down the road, both financially and mentally.

—⁓—

Miscellaneous

It's the little things that add up to make a big impact on your budget. If you save a nickel or a dime here and there, over time, you will see results.

Being frugal and aware of your spending is a mind-set. It is a habit that is profitable.

Buy used and save. When you are buying clothes and household goods, get in the habit of shopping at thrift stores and garage sales. You can buy items for a tenth of the retail price. You can even find furniture and other items you may need free at http://www.freecycle.org. It's easy to use Freecycle, and you also help save the planet by keeping stuff out of the landfill. You can also find great bargains at Craigslist.org. The idea behind using these online sources to buy your possessions is to avoid the high markups for new items in retail shops. If you save money in the process, you have less need to work for money, or it will be less of a strain on your nest egg.

A way to save money on tools and equipment is to borrow the items from your friends, neighbors, or family. If you need a chainsaw, borrow it instead of buying one. If you bought a chainsaw, you would most likely use it only one or two times, and you have to store it. There is a website for borrowing items that might be available in your area: http://neighborgoods. net. It is not widespread yet; however, you can start your own neighborhood group using this website. Its tagline is "save money and resources by sharing stuff with your friends." If you can't find someone to share an item, then rent your tool from a local rental store at a reasonable price. You can find all kinds of power tools and equipment to rent by the hour or day.

If you need to repair something in your house, sometimes it's best to have a professional do the job. You may come out ahead when you consider avoiding costly mistakes you could make yourself. You could also save a lot of time. However, don't be afraid to do your own repair jobs if the fix is relatively straightforward. You can find a number of books and CDs at the library that can show you how to do the job and save on labor costs. You can also find videos on YouTube.com that can demonstrate step-by-step instructions. Another idea is to find friends, family, or neighbors who have skills to do the job in exchange for something you have in your garage that you are willing to give away. You might also be able to exchange skills, such as trading your accounting services for an acquaintance's plumbing expertise.

If you still have hair, it needs to be cut once in a while. Having your spouse or friend trim your hair saves money. You can also go to a hairstyling school and have the students cut your hair. You can also color your hair at home to save big. Counting income taxes, you can save hundreds per year.

Finally, there are books, such as *The Tightwad Gazette*, by Amy Dacyczyn, that have hundreds of money-saving ideas and tips. Many are small savings, but remember that a little here and a little there really adds up.

—∿—

Charity

It feels great to give. Average American households give a little over 3 percent of their income to charity. It is essential to try to make the world a better place for those less fortunate. If you retired broke, then you probably don't have any extra money to give away. Instead, find ways to give your time. You should have a lot of spare time in your retirement, and donating time is just as helpful as money. You can volunteer at the local food bank each week for a few hours. If you donate sixteen hours a week, it's like giving $12,480 per year. That is based on an income of $15 per hour. That is money you don't have to earn from a job or take out of your nest egg. If you need to drive to the charity, your mileage may be deductible on your tax return.

Where to begin if you don't have a favorite cause? You can go to http://www.volunteermatch.org to find something close to your heart. As of 2014, the website claims to have matched more than eight million volunteers with about one hundred thousand participating organizations. You can search for causes involving advocacy and human rights, animals, arts, veterans, and seniors, just to name a few.

Part III

Income Options

If you have reduced your expenses as much as you can and you still find that you cannot stay afloat, then you may need to generate a source of income to make ends meet. At least you won't need as much income as you did before you found ways to cut your overhead. This means you can get by with a smaller nest egg, start your own small business, or even just take a part-time job. These are the three main methods to generate the income you need for retirement. If you have very expensive tastes and live the high life, or if you are so far in debt that the methods in this book don't solve your problems, then you may not have any choice but to look for another full-time job or stay with the job you already have for another five to ten years—or more.

When you have the freedom to choose to do what you want with your life, you may find yourself much happier. If you are a slave to expensive desires, you can be forced to remain in a job you hate. Even worse, you may find yourself over your head in debt and experiencing all the stress that comes with it. Reducing our expensive desires and being happy with the free or nearly free things around us is freedom.

The following are some ideas to generate additional income when Social Security, pensions, and reducing your overhead aren't sufficient.

Earning Income from Your Investments

If you happen to have a nest egg, congratulations. Remember, one-third of all retirees don't have any retirement savings. What is the best way to invest your nest egg? Ninety percent of investors should manage their own money. Managing your own investments can seem intimidating, but it doesn't have to be. Do it yourself, and save on the high fees investment managers charge for their services. Some think it's fine because it's only 1 percent. That's not much, right? Think again. It can be substantial. With a 1 percent management fee, a high-cost mutual fund (fees up to 1.5 percent), and turnover costs, you could be spending up to 3 percent for professional money management.

How much might it cost you with only 2 percent in fees? Let's take a portfolio of 60 percent stocks and 40 percent bonds, in which the value of the nest egg is $100,000. This was the average portfolio size for one-third of retirees in 2012. Let's assume you turn your money over to an investment advisor, who promises to manage your money for you. He or she charges a 1 percent management fee on the balance of your portfolio and has you invested in active mutual funds that have an average 1 percent fee for investing with them. That is a total of 2 percent, which is on the low side. Many retirees pay more than that amount. Let's assume you don't need the money just yet since you are going to live off your Social Security income and a small pension. You let the money grow for fifteen years. This portfolio mix will generate about 6.7 percent return over this time with the current low bond rates. How much will you have with a 2 percent management fee reducing your investments returns over fifteen years? Perhaps you will have $199,159 after fees. You almost doubled your money! Not bad, you say. What would have happened if you had managed your investments yourself?

If you invest with the same 60/40 mix with the stock portion invested in low-cost index funds, you could get your management cost down to .002 percent, which is one-tenth the cost of having someone else doing it for you. What would the balance be in fifteen years? Assuming everything is the same except for the fees, it would be $257,184 after the lower fees. That is $58,025 extra in your pocket. That is 29 percent more money. Is it worth having somebody hold your hand? Or can you do it yourself? Or course, your results will be less if you have to spend income from your investments on the first day of your retirement instead of letting it grow over fifteen years. For example taking $4,000 income the first year and increasing the income by three percent inflation each year will leave you with $133,781 ending balance. However with a 2 percent management fee the same income option will leave you with $92,335. You still benefit substantially when managing the portfolio yourself by avoiding the management fees.

Some investors love the idea of managing their own money. They say, "Keep your hands off of it; it's mine." However, some people are terrified about watching over their own nest egg. If you are one of these people, you shouldn't be scared. It's rather easy if you do passive investing instead of active management. What if you don't know a thing about investing in stocks? There is a short primer for beginners at http://www.investopedia.com/university/beginner.

If you still feel that you would rather have somebody manage your money on your behalf, the best way, in our opinion, is with a company called Wealthfront. The company's website, http://www.wealthfront.com, states, "Wealthfront is the world's largest and fastest-growing automated investment service with over $1 billion in client assets. We manage a diversified, continually rebalanced portfolio of index funds on your behalf at a very low cost and in an extremely tax efficient manner." The company charges a quarter of 1 percent for managing your money, investing in low-cost index funds similar to what we outline next in passive investing. That is $250 per year on a $100,000 portfolio.

Now, back to passive investing. What exactly is it? You buy a total of six index funds that charge less than .002 percent fees, and you are set. About once a year, you rebalance your funds. So, you are spending less than four hours per year on your investments.

What is rebalancing? When you set up your portfolio, you decide on how much money to put into each of the six funds. This is your allocation. Once a year, you sell part of the funds that exceed their allocation and buy more of the funds that have fallen below your target allocation. For example, you started with 60 percent stocks and 40 percent bonds. At the end of the year, your stocks grow in value to 70 percent of your portfolio, changing the bond allocation to 30 percent. You simply sell part of your stocks and reinvest in the bonds to bring your allocation back to a 60/40 mix.

What are these six funds?

The first fund is a total market index of US stocks, which will have your large companies, midsize companies, small companies, and value and growth type stocks all mixed into one fund. You could get fancy and buy an index fund for each of these categories to tweak the allocation and increase the expected rate of return. For example, heavier investments into small-cap and value stocks will increase your rate of return. Another option is to keep it simple and buy one fund with everything already mixed. The suggested allocation is 25 percent to 30 percent of the stock portion of your portfolio.

The second fund, international, is simply the same mix of stock types but is invested in stocks overseas. It's best not to have over 30 percent of your stock portion invested in the international class.

The third fund is emerging countries. These are stocks in countries with fast-growing economies. They are considered more volatile because they sometimes fluctuate wildly, so it's best to keep this allocation to between 5 and 10 percent.

The fourth fund is REITs. This is real estate. The acronym stands for Real Estate Investment Trust. It is simply a fund that invests in all kinds of real estate, such as office buildings, apartments, strip malls, and rental storage spaces. You can buy a fund that specializes in one of these real estate investments or invest in a fund that has a mixed collection of many types of real estate. It is best to keep your REIT allocation to about 10 percent of the stock portion of your portfolio.

The fifth fund is natural resources, which are investments in raw materials that are used in the production of finished goods. They range from metals such as copper and gold to oil and gas and include materials that are used for farming, such as fertilizer. It is best to buy an index fund that invests in many types of natural resources. Keep the allocation to about 5 percent of your stock portion of your portfolio.

Finally, the last fund is a total bond fund, which invests in all types of bonds with a mix of federal bonds and corporate bonds. It will also have a mix of safety ratings, from low-risk to high-risk bonds. The bond fund will also have bonds with varying lengths of duration, from one year or less to thirty-year bonds. You buy a total bond fund that has a mix of everything. The percentage you allocate to bonds will determine how volatile your portfolio will be. The more you have in bonds, the less your portfolio fluctuates, but you will earn less return over time. Most people in or near retirement can tolerate anywhere from 35 to 65 percent of their total portfolio in bonds. You know that you have found the right mix of bonds and stocks if you can fall asleep easily at night. Keep in mind that when interest rates go up, the value of your bonds go down, so you can lose money in a bond fund. If you feel that interest rates are going up substantially, you can invest your funds temporarily for one to five years in CDs at the bank. You will avoid capital losses during a prolonged rate hike. Keep in mind that the CDs will be insured in the bank for up to $250,000. If you have more than this in your bond portion of your allocation, then you need to use more than one bank.

If you stay with low-cost index funds offered by Vanguard, Fidelity, and Charles Schwab, you will find what you need to fill your six slots. There are a number of books on index investing you can check out at the library; some will suggest specific funds to buy. Anything written by Larry E. Swedroe is an excellent place to start. He has a book on index investing called *The Only Guide You'll Ever Need for the Right Financial Plan.* Another good book on the subject is *Index Funds: The 12-Step Recovery Program for Active Investors*, by Mark Hebner.

Sound easy? It is. You can open an account with a discount broker-age company, such as Fidelity, Scottrade, or Vanguard. You can search for other companies if those don't suit you. Choose a company that charges low commission fees, has low minimum balance requirements, and will allow you to withdraw your funds without any fees. It's easy to transfer your total nest egg account from one company to another. The brokers will help you.

There is one brokerage company that is really doing it right: Motif Investing (http://www.motifinvesting.com). The company allows you to buy up to thirty stocks or ETF index funds all at once for a one-time fee of only $9.95. This can save you hundreds on commissions over time. When your portfolio allocations get out of whack, you can rebal-ance your account to your original fixed allocation by simply buying another Motif portfolio with your six index funds. You can do it in a few minutes and at a cost of less than $10 per year. Since it's so cheap, you could even rebalance once per quarter, but for most, once a year should be enough.

Why passive investing instead of active investing? Passive investing is simply matching the returns of the market minus your fees, and your index portfolio will outperform at least 80 percent of those trying to beat the market over a ten-year period. Those folks work so hard being active investors and spend hundreds of hours researching and monitoring the markets, yet the majority still can't do better than the passive investor. We would rather sit back, relax, and do more useful things with our time. Remember, it takes only about a half a day per year to monitor your investments. You don't have to spend countless hours researching individual companies to purchase and don't have to try profiting on short-term price fluctuations, which is why it's called passive investing.

Over a ten- to fifteen-year period, passive investing could generate about a 9.6 percent annual return on the stock allocation part of your portfolio. When you include a bond allocation of forty to sixty percent of the total portfolio to reduce the volatility, the returns on the total portfolio will be lower, around 5.3 percent to 6.2 percent with today's bond rate environment. If bonds return to normal rates not influenced by the government, then the total return will be higher.

So what if you are not satisfied with the market averages? You want to try to beat the market and shoot for the stars with higher returns. The odds are slim—there is only a 20 percent chance of outperforming the market over ten years. We wouldn't recommend the average investor try to do it, but if you insist, we'll show you how. Part of it is luck. Part of it is by following one or more of the five methods of increasing returns:

1. Time the market.
2. Use leverage.
3. Pick individual stocks instead of index funds.
4. Hire a manager who picks stocks for you. Active mutual funds fall in that camp.
5. Maintain a concentrated portfolio of stocks, such as nine stocks instead of hundreds of securities.

Timing the market and trying to switch from stocks to cash or bonds just before the market declines is a fool's game. Nobody can do it consistently over time. If they could, they would have all the money in the world eventually. Avoid the con artist that sells you an online newsletter or service that claims to inform you when to time the markets. If he or she really could do it, he or she would invest his or her own money and make more profits timing the market themselves than trying to sell (empty) promises online. As a passive investor, it's best just to hold on to your investments over a long period of time. When you rebalance your portfolio, you are timing the market in a way, but it's a sane way. You are selling high and buying low when rebalancing your passive funds, which increases your profits.

Using leverage is risky. This is borrowing money using your stocks as collateral. If the market crashes, you could lose all your investments. And when you factor in the cost of paying the interest, you may not be coming out ahead that much. It's not worth it. The only time we might consider using leverage is when the market has already crashed. If the market has already declined by 40 to 50 percent, you may want to buy as much stock as possible at bargain prices. That is when leverage might be useful, but those opportunities don't come around very often. If they do, use only a small amount of leverage, if any, and only for a short period of time.

Picking individual stocks can increase your returns, but it can be riskier than investing in a passive index fund. It takes a great deal of time to research and monitor individual stocks. Remember, the professional stock pickers are on the same playing field, doing the same thing you are doing. It's like playing a professional football game against the Seattle Seahawks. Most likely, you don't have a chance. Why try? It could be fun picking your own stocks and watching them soar in value. If you feel convinced that one or two companies you have been watching will become the next Walmart, then you might be all right buying a few shares as a side bet in addition to your index funds. We have bought a few shares of a technology stock, but it is not part of our passive index portfolio. Instead, we consider it as a long-term side bet that might pay off in fifteen to twenty years.

Paying someone else to pick your investments includes paying up to a 1.5 percent fee to a mutual fund, which might be a way to increase your returns. But we already know that only a small percentage of active managers beat the market over a ten-year period. You may find people who can do it for a few years, but over ten years, they eventually lose all of their excess gains, and the market averages beat them.

Having a concentrated portfolio of stocks, such as having only nine stocks, can increase your returns. It can also set you back by a large percentage if one or two of the stocks take a big dive. With index investing, you have automatic diversification. The index funds can have thousands of stocks. If one stock goes bust, it won't affect you much in the grand scheme of things.

That is a brief summary of what investing can do for you. We would like to leave you with an important thought. If you know that you will be using all of your nest egg within the next few years, then you shouldn't participate in the stock market. Instead, keep your money invested in CDs with different time frames based on your expected budget forecast. Stock investments need at least ten years—fifteen years is preferable—for the index market averages to work in your favor. If you are spending your nest egg within five years and it is invested in the stock market, the risk of a market decline could wipe you out, and you can't afford to lose that money. If you have ten to fifteen years, you can ride out a market decline in most cases with no problem if you are not withdrawing too much income from your nest egg. Try keeping it sensible—in the 3.5 percent to 4.5 percent range—if you need to withdraw funds for your retirement.

—⚒—

Part-Time Work

According to a Gallup Poll conducted April 4–14, 2013, three-quarters of the working population plan on working past retirement age. Forty percent plan to keep working by choice because they love their jobs, but thirty-five percent plan to work by necessity because they don't have enough money saved for retirement. Nineteen percent will stop working by choice, three percent will stop working by necessity, and one percent of those surveyed had no opinion.

Because of health reasons or because they desire a flexible schedule to engage in hobbies, traveling, or spending time with their grandkids, many will choose part-time employment. If you plan on collecting Social Security income early—age sixty-two is the earliest age to start—then you are limited to the amount of income you can earn from a job before it reduces your Social Security benefits. For tax year 2015, the limit is $15,720. For every two dollars you make over this limit during the year, your benefits are reduced by one dollar. However, you recapture the lost money with higher benefits when you reach full retirement age. It is gradually added to your monthly check to repay you over time. Keep in mind that once you reach full retirement age, there is no limit to the amount of income you can earn, and there will be no reduction in Social Security payments.

Income from a part-time job could save your retirement. If you earned $15,720 for the year, it is like having a $393,000 nest egg with a standard 4 percent withdrawal rate. If you have reduced your overhead by quite a bit, then $15,720 will go a long way toward paying for essentials.

How do you go about looking for a part-time job these days? The first step is to contact your former boss if you are still on good terms. He or she may have leads at your old company that could connect you with a part-time opportunity. You can ask your friends and family for leads as well. Start an account at LinkedIn.com, which is a business-oriented social media site used primarily for professional networking. You can post on your profile that you are looking for part-time employment. There may be a number of recruiters who will find you based on your intentions. Be sure your profile includes any skills and work experience you have; LinkedIn will send you e-mails when job openings that fit any of the skills you have listed are posted. There is also a job search section on the site that lists job opportunities. You can join this site for free, although a more robust service is offered for a small fee.

If you are over the age of fifty, you can try websites designed for older workers, such as the US Department of State's (http://www.state.gov/m/fsi/tc/79977.htm), which lists twenty-one different websites where you can search for job opportunities. Other useful sites are http://www.workforce50.com and http://www.employmentspot.com.

Some are still using traditional employment websites, such as Monster.com and Careerbuilder.com, for job leads. Don't forget to use temp services, also known as staffing companies. You can search for temp agencies in your area. There are a number of small temp agencies. However, there are three companies that we know have a national presence and a good reputation: Kelly Services, Manpower, and Accountemps.

If you have a skill such as web development, graphic design, marketing, or writing, you can freelance your services on Elance.com, which adds an 8.75 percent fee to your price for use of its website. You can also check out guru.com to freelance your skills. Flexjobs.com is another source to find telecommuting, part-time, and freelance work. The company charges $14.95 per month for their services.

If you would like to travel while you work, check out http://www.cool-works.com/older-bolder. You may find a job as a cook on a cruise ship, work in a national park, or something at a fancy resort in a popular vacation destination.

Craigslist.org also posts part-time jobs in its classified section. They tend to be low-paying jobs, but this may come in handy if you are unable to find work elsewhere. Stay away from work-at-home schemes advertised online that seem too good to be true. They tend to be scams, and you could waste your time and money on them.

Finally, you could turn your hobby into a part-time job, which we will cover in the next chapter.

Starting a Business on a Shoestring

You may find yourself in a situation in which finding someone willing to hire you seems impossible. Your skills are outdated. Your age may be a turn-off. You have no network to tap into for job opportunities. There can be any number of reasons why it may be difficult to find a job. Maybe you can find a job, but it doesn't pay enough. Maybe you have to drive too far for the job, or maybe the hours conflict with your family life, school, or other obligations. What might work instead? Starting your own business.

Think small. Really small. Start-up costs can run into the hundreds of thousands if you start with a large business. Doing so can also be too risky. Here is a story to illustrate how big may not be best.

Joe wanted to run a large lawn-mowing service in the Midwest, which has a seven-month mowing season. He wanted it to be big. Really big. He spent $12,000 for five trailers to haul around ten lawn mowers that cost $10,000 each. They had to be the fancy commercial kind that you can turn on a dime and stand up on it as it moves. That cost him $112,000. Then, he had to lease five trucks to haul the trailers at a cost of $36,000 per year. Then, there was the cost of maintenance and the cost of gas. Also, he had to hire thirteen employees and keep them happy enough to stay with him. Every time someone quit, there was a turnover cost to hire and train someone new. There were warehouse rental fees to store all the equipment and trucks. An office and staff were needed to keep track of all the customers and the money, the employees, payroll and taxes, insurance, and maintenance. He needed over $150,000 to begin this business the first year, and that didn't even pay for the employee's salaries. Those ran at least $160,000 for the seven-month season for wages of $10 per hour plus FICA taxes. He had to mow about four thousand lawns for the season just to break even on the labor cost alone. Remember, he had to mow additional lawns to cover the other overhead cost and pay down the start-up costs. When paying for everything to support the overhead in his business, Joe's company had to mow eighty-one hundred lawns per year, or about forty-five lawns per day. Think of the ulcers, the headaches, the responsibilities, and possible labor lawsuits or replacement of damaged sprinkler systems damaged by his crew. He also had to advertise. He ended up making about $5,000 profit the first year, spinning his wheels.

Small can be beautiful, and there is an easier way to do it. Work only for yourself. No employees. No warehouse. Work from home. You can even do without the trailer and leased truck. Just knock on a couple of dozen doors in your neighborhood, and drag your push mower next door and mow. There's no overhead cost to speak of. You might get seven or eight customers within walking distance of your house. If you charge $40 per lawn, you'll have about $304 per week after gas. That is a $9,120 profit for a seven-month season. You almost double the profits with fewer headaches and less work compared with Joe's nightmare story above. You have to work only about eight hours per week. No ulcers, no headaches. And you don't have to worry about an employee suing you over some silly misunderstanding about how he is getting paid. It is a lean business that you can start for less than $500.

Granted, $9,120 will only pay part of your bills for the year. That is the reason you might need to have two or three other small businesses to complete the rest of your yearly income. Some of your businesses may be seasonal. You work one in the winter and the other during the summer. Maybe you only work during the tourist season when your small town swells up with a number of people who will be your customers. Another reason to have more than one business is that if one business slows down, another one may pick up. Try to have at least two businesses going at once. You can shovel snow in the winter for the same neighbors you mowed lawns for during the summer. It doesn't take much profit from your two or three small businesses to support yourself if you are following some of the other ideas in this book to reduce your living expenses. In your new stage in life, you may want more time for yourself to do the things you want to do. You may not want to be tied down to a full-time, big operation and all of the stress that comes with it.

Most small-scale businesses are providing services for somebody. Cleaning houses, walking dogs, handyman work, home care for seniors, and mowing lawns are just a few of the many ideas for your business. We're sure you will be able to think of something that fits your personality and skills. Your primary marketing will be done with Craigslist, a free website that has a classified advertising section where you can offer the services your company provides. Some money may be required for tools and supplies, but try not to accumulate debt. Debt is a burden that saps your resources. You have no retail space to rent and no outside office to maintain. You work from your home office to keep track of your receipts, invoices, and taxes. It is your base of operations. There is lower overhead all around.

What kind of businesses could we start for less than $500? Here is a list to get you started:

Pooper scooper: Dog waste removal from the backyards of people's houses.

Dog walker or sitter: Must love pets.

Mow lawns: Will need to use the mower you already have.

Handyman services: Must be good with your hands and have your own tools.

Babysitting: Must like kids. Babysit too many at a time, though, and you may need a license.

Clean houses or offices: You can charge by the hour or by the half day.

Detail cars: Might be able to sell your services to used car dealerships.

Clean gutters or hang Christmas lights on houses: Must not be afraid of heights. Having your own ladder is a plus for homeowners.

Landscaping: Do you have a green thumb? Again, having your own tools is a plus.

Snow removal: It would be much easier if you had a snowblower; see if you can buy one used, which will be much cheaper than new.

Music lessons (voice, piano, or guitar): Do you have talent and an instrument?

Painting houses: Some experience and your own equipment (ladders, drop sheets, brushes, etc.) would be helpful.

Errand runner: Must be organized and keep track of your mileage.

Organize garages, basements, attics: Must enjoy organizing and purging. It might also help to be unafraid of spiders and mice.

Freelance writing (for magazines or local papers): Some experience is usually necessary.

Photography: Helps if you already have a nice camera and know how to use it.

Design websites: If you have the desire but no experience, take community college classes to learn the latest technology.

Tour guide: Must love your area and know it like the back of your hand.

Personal shopper: If you love to shop and are stylish, this could be right up your alley.

At first, most of your time should be spent drumming up business. You will be knocking on doors, making phone calls, and putting up signs around the neighborhood. You may get enough business just from Craigslist, so it may be easier than you expect. Later, you will get repeat business from a roster of customers you retain. You may even get referrals from your other customers.

How It's Done: An Example

Sam just lost his job. He's sixty-two years old. He was planning to work to age sixty-eight to save more money and add to his $100,000 nest egg, but his employer had other ideas. The company outsourced Sam's job overseas to increase profits at his expense. His wife, Sally, the same age, lost her job last year and has been unable to find another one. They don't have enough assets or income to support them in an early retirement. What are they going to do to survive? How are they going to create the retirement life they dream about?

Instead of panicking, they sit down together and work out a plan. They construct a budget to reflect the lifestyle they want. They keep it simple and keep their expectations low. Next, they determine how much money will be coming in to support their budgeted items. They don't have pensions, but both decide to start receiving their Social Security benefits early. Combined, they will receive $30,000 per year. Sam also has a lead on a part-time job he found online that will earn him $6,000 per year. They also have $4,000 coming from their nest egg. That's $40,000 income to support their lifestyle.

However, their projected yearly budget is $60,000. They are short $20,000. If they had saved more money when they were younger, they could have had an additional $500,000 in their nest egg to generate the $20,000 they need to close the gap. Now, they have to find a way to cut $20,000 from their budget. Oh, by the way, they still have $8,000 in credit card debt, and the payments are not included in their budget. Might now be the time to panic? Not yet.

They read this book and pick out the options they want to try for reducing their overhead. They write down the steps to take and the goals they want to achieve. Having both the budget and a written plan of what actions to take gives them a sense that things are going to work out and that they will be OK.

The next step they take is to sell Sam's motorcycle to pay off half the debt. He doesn't ride anymore since his best friend was killed in a motorcycle accident last year. The other half of the debt will be paid off by holding several garage sales and selling items like Sally's Precious Moments collectibles and Sam's coin collection on eBay. They want to declutter their life anyway, so they might as well do it profitably and make their credit card debt disappear. Now they don't have to worry about earning income to pay credit card payments, but they are still $20,000 behind in their budget. What's next?

Their kids moved out of the house several years ago and are on their own with successful careers. Sam and Sally's house will be paid off in five years. They feel like the house is too big for them with three extra bedrooms, but they love their home and don't want to downsize or move across the country to a less expensive area as we suggested in this book. They have friends nearby, and their kids still live in town. They know grandkids will be in the picture someday. So, they decide to rent out one of their bedrooms for $600 a month to a college student attending the local school. Sam knows they will rent out part of their home for only five years until the mortgage is paid in full. When the loan is paid off, the money saved on mortgage payments will make up for the lost rental income. It will be just in time to reclaim their bedroom for any grandkids who want to stay with Grandma and Grandpa. This step will generate $7,200 per year. Now they are only $12,800 short to support their budget.

Sam and Sally decided to sell one of their two cars and get by with just one. The proceeds are used to pay off a car loan with a couple of hundred dollars to spare. They still budget for the $250 monthly car payment, but they deposit that amount into a bank account instead. Even though they will try to keep the remaining car running until the odometer hits two hundred thousand miles, they know they will have to replace it eventually. The mock car payments will yield them enough to buy another car someday. They are still short $12,800 on their budget, but the reduced insurance, property taxes, and other related savings from getting rid of an extra car saves $700 per year. They also have an extra garage space to rent out for $75 per month ($900 per year) to a neighbor who needs to store his boat. These two factors now cut $1,600 from their yearly budget. Now their budget shortfall is only $11,200.

The couple shopped for health insurance on the Affordable Health Care site, and the payments are reflected in their new retirement budget. In three years, they will be on Medicare.

Since Sally has to take prescriptions regularly for a chronic condition, she asks her doctor to prescribe generic drugs. Some of her pills can be split in half to save money. She also orders a three-month supply through the mail. These steps save her $2,000 per year on her prescriptions. Now the budget shortfall is only $9,200.

Both spouses replace their eyeglasses every two years: Sam in odd years and Sally in even years. They order online, which saves them $700 per year. Now they still need to find a way to cut $8,500 from their overhead.

Sam decides now is the time to quit smoking. He has already tried three times in the past to quit, but now he is determined to do it. He found the advice for breaking bad habits helpful along with the smoking cessation patches his doctor prescribed. He was a chain smoker who smoked a pack a day. Quitting smoking generates a yearly savings of $2,000. The couple can now see the light at the end of the tunnel since there is only a $6,500 shortfall.

For their food budget, they decide to eat out less often. When they do eat out, they split an entrée, drink water instead of soft drinks, and skip dessert. They also entertain friends with home-cooked meals instead of eating out, using produce from their own garden. They freeze the surplus for the winter months. They also decide to eat less meat by having vegetarian meals three nights a week. With all of the money-saving strategies for food, they save $2,500 per year. Now they are looking at only a $4,000 deficit with their yearly budget.

So far, they have cut a total of $16,000 per year from their budget. They need to cut $20,000. Guess what? They have already hit their goal of saving the full $20,000 because they do not have to pay taxes on money they don't spend; the $4,000 shortfall is covered by savings on income tax expenses. Look what happens when you think smarter and have a plan. Your options open up, and your life becomes more flexible.

Sam and Sally are now confident that they can survive with their unexpected new lifestyle. They can live on a $40,000 budget instead of a $60,000 one. The Social Security income, part-time job, and income from their small nest egg supports their retirement. If they want to supercharge it even more, they could rent to two roommates instead of one and save the extra $7,200 for their nest egg or spend the money on traveling or hobbies. It's definitely something to think about.

Once they figure out how to manage their budget items, Sally starts thinking about the traveling she and Sam always thought they would do once they finished working. Everyone she knows says she is a great cook, and she really enjoys preparing food for people to eat, so she checks out coolworks.com to see if there are any seasonal cooking jobs that would help her realize her dream. Sam's job as a school crossing guard near their home will allow him to travel during the summers, and if he can find work at the same resorts as Sally, that will help pay for their travels. He wonders if his fly-fishing experience will be useful.

—⚉—

Example Two

In the previous example, we showed a typical married couple with $100,000 in savings and $40,000 income, which represents the one-third of retirees in the United States who have underfunded retirements but some savings. What about another third of retirees, those who are without much of any-thing—retired broke?

Meet Rhonda. She was forced to retire this year at age sixty-six from an eighteen-year career in customer service. She was making $18.65 per hour, which translated into a $38,820 annual income. She was just able to cover her living expenses on this salary. However, now during retirement, her only source of income will be Social Security, which is only $15,528 per year. Her employer didn't offer a pension, and she never felt she could afford to con-tribute to a 401(k). She's worried now about how to survive on 40 percent less income. She has zero savings and no money waiting for her in an IRA account. She is almost at the federal poverty line, which is $11,670 for a one-person household.

Rhonda is single, living alone in a one-bedroom apartment that rents for $775 per month. This represented 24 percent of her previous salary, which was doable. But now with only her Social Security, her one-bedroom apartment is costing her almost 60 percent of her income. She can't afford it and knows she needs to make some drastic changes in her life to survive. How is she going to do it?

Housing. Friends suggested Rhonda look into HUD housing assis-tance. She can qualify for a rent-assisted apartment because she is over age sixty and because the median income in her area is high. However, there is one problem. She is on a four-year waiting list for assistance. What is she going to do in the meantime? Faced with this dilemma, she settles on a very creative solution. She decides to house-sit for folks who need someone to watch over their houses and tend to plants and pets. She joins http://www.mindmyhouse.com/index.php/ to find suitable assignments within five hundred miles of her hometown. This is close enough to allow her to drive to assignments within one day without incurring hotel costs. The assignments last anywhere from two weeks to six months. In the event that she needs a place to stay for a few days between assignments, her sister has room for her to stay. They enjoy each other's company, and Rhonda earns her keep by helping out with chores around the house. Rhonda's sister and brother-in-law have suggested she stay up to a month if needed, but it may not be necessary because she plans to stay busy with her house-sitting jobs. She does make an important decision that helps with this transition. She pares down her possessions to almost nothing, allowing her to travel light to her assignments and not impose on her sister with tons of stuff. The cost of housing is zero. The money remaining in her budget to spend is still $15,528.

Health Care. Rhonda qualifies for Medicare. She spends $200 per month for Medicare supplemental insurance plus an additional $130 for Part B and D of Medicare. She is relatively healthy, taking only one generic prescription for high blood pressure, which she buys for only $4 per month at Walmart. After paying for copays, prescriptions, and insurance, her health care costs are only $4,658 per year, which represents 30 percent of her income. Her remaining budget is $10,870.

Transportation. Her car is paid for, so she has no car payments. However, she is putting $100 per month into savings to eventually have enough money to replace her car with a good, dependable used one. She figures that in about six years, she will have $7,500 to spend. She drives ten thousand miles a year. Transportation costs equal $4,600 per year, which is also 30 percent of her income. Her remaining budget is $6,270.

Food. Rhonda doesn't qualify for SNAP benefits (previously known as food stamps). She also doesn't qualify for the local food pantry because she made $275 too much money for the year and is required to have a permanent address. She falls between the cracks. However, she makes all of her meals from scratch with basic food purchases such as dry beans, rice, cheese, eggs, and oatmeal. Rhonda shops mostly at the deep discount grocery stores such as Aldi. Her monthly food budget is $63 per week, which averages out to $3 per meal. Her food cost equals $3,276 per year, or 21 percent of her income. Her remaining budget is $2,994.

Insurance. Because of her lifestyle, she has no need for life insurance or homeowner's insurance. Her only insurance costs are car insurance, which is included in the transportation portion of her budget, and her MediGap insurance, which is included in the health portion of her budget. Her remaining budget is still $2,994.

Taxes. Rhonda doesn't make enough money to pay any income taxes. However, she needs to pay a small amount in self-employment tax because of a small jewelry making business she started after retirement. She pays this out of her profits. Her remaining budget is still $2,994.

Debt. Rhonda has no debt. She has lived frugally and responsibly, which has helped her credit score. Her high credit score helped her to purchase her car insurance at a fairly low price.

Having fun. Her entertainment cost is virtually zero because most of the houses she watches over have cable TV and Internet service. She reads a lot of books for free from the library. She has no pet costs since she no longer has a dog in her life, but she often interacts with the pets the owners leave behind when she house-sits. Her remaining budget is still $2,994.

Bad Habits. Rhonda has no bad habits except for purchasing an occasional lottery ticket, which comes out of the miscellaneous portion of her budget. The money remaining in her budget? Still $2,994.

Miscellaneous. The remaining $2,994 is spent on personal items such as toiletries, haircuts, and the other little things that make for a pleasant life. This also includes a low-cost cell phone plan and a small budget for buying gifts for her nieces and nephews.

Charity. Rhonda gives no money to charity; however, she volunteers at the food bank near her sister's house when she is in town. She figures her time equals about $2,000 worth of free labor. This amounts to about 10 percent of her annual income.

Self-employment income. Rhonda is still living on the edge since she has no savings for expenses such as replacing her cell phone every few years or for dental costs and eyeglasses that are not covered by Medicare. She may still encounter other unexpected expenses that pop up occasionally. She has always enjoyed making jewelry and decides to use her hobby to make a little extra money by selling her creations in gift shops. She tried selling her handcrafted items on several Internet sites but was not successful because of intense competition and underpricing practices by other artists. However, she has a niece that owns a gift shop in a tourist destination on the East Coast who is willing to sell Rhonda's jewelry for a 40 percent commission. Rhonda also has her jewelry on consignment in a gift shop near her sister's house that specializes in items made by local artists. With only these two outlets for selling her art, she is able to make about $2,500 net profit after paying for materials, shipping, and other expenses. This keeps her below the level that federal and state income taxes are required, but she will still need to pay about $382 for self-employment taxes. She works on her hobby for only an hour or two per day while house-sitting. All of her supplies and materials can be transported from place to place with a simple toolbox. She figures she is only making about $7.50 per hour, which isn't much, but the $2,500 per year helps her pay for any extras she needs to stay afloat. She would do her hobby for nothing since she enjoys creating jewelry, so it's a bonus that she makes money from it. If she needs more money, she could put more effort and hours into making jewelry, but she will be required to pay federal and state income taxes above the $2,500 profit level.

As you can see with Rhonda's creative solution to her housing dilemma and her hobby turned self-employment, she is able to enjoy her retirement. She gets to see and explore other places as she travels to her house-sitting assignments. Rhonda can still enjoy life with simple pleasures that don't cost much. Her hobby pays her a little income, and she enjoys creating art. Her life is never boring since she is in a new place every few months.

Conclusion

If you find yourself in an underfunded retirement, we hope some of the ideas offered in this book will help you manage your situation. Remember, the first step is to write down your goals. What do you want your retirement to look like? A budget is important because it's useful to see where you are going and to assess what funds you have available to work with. If there is something you want to happen in your retirement, but a lack of money is an obstacle, sometimes the best resource is your own creative ideas. You just think smarter and find a different way to obtain the same objective with little or no money. One example is the European vacation you have while house-sitting for someone in London. You still have to figure out the transportation cost, but the hotel cost just evaporated, making the whole adventure more affordable.

When you draft your original budget and find that you can cut it by one-third just by following some of the cost-cutting ideas in Part II of this book, it can reduce the need for cash. Reducing your budget outlays is almost the same as having a nest egg earning you cash. You are not doing without, just finding ways to do the same with less.

If you cut your budget and still find you are short of cash, a part-time job or self-employment may be an additional step needed to secure your retirement. A budget that has been cut to two-thirds of its original size may allow you to work less.

However, sometimes your situation is so dire that you may need to drastically change your lifestyle. Moving across the country, living in another country, or taking in roommates are just some examples. Life is an adventure, and turning it upside down can bring you experiences you may find fulfilling, such as new friendships, new surroundings, or a new passion. More important, you will find a way to survive an underfunded retirement.

Appendix: How to Avoid the 10 Percent Penalty from an IRA Withdrawal

Did you cash out 100 percent of your traditional IRA or 401(k) when you needed the money? That could have been a big mistake. If you are under the age of fifty-nine and a half, you may be subject to a 10 percent penalty on top of income taxes you have to pay. If you withdraw funds in the same year that you left your job, it could also push you into a higher tax bracket, which could be another 10 percent hit or more. When you factor in the early withdrawal penalty and the higher taxes, you could lose close to half of your money if you take it out all at once. For example, you had $50,000 saved up in your IRA and took it all out. You might have to pay close to $20,000 to the tax man, leaving you with only about $30,000. We can show you how to save yourself more than half of that tax hit. You could use the extra cash for your retirement.

Of course, some people may be in a desperate situation and will take that 40 percent tax hit just to survive. Before doing something so drastic, try following some of the other ideas in this book to see if it will be enough to get you back on your feet before you destroy your IRA or 401(k).

There is a way to avoid the 10 percent penalty. It is a little-known secret called a 72(t) election. It is allowed by the IRS for folks who wish to retire before the age of fifty-nine and a half. With this option, you must take an equal periodic withdrawal for at least five years or until you reach age fifty-nine and a half, whichever is the longest period of time. You may have to go past age fifty-nine and a half if you start less than five years before you reach that age. For example, if you started the withdrawals at age fifty-six, then you must withdraw an equal amount each year until you are age sixty-one. Once you reach your age target, you are allowed to withdraw any amount you wish, and the 10 percent penalty no longer applies; however, you must still pay income tax.

Keep in mind that once you start a 72(t) election, you cannot stop or change the amount of withdrawal. If you do, the IRS will require you to go back and pay the 10 percent penalty for each year you made the withdrawal that you were under the age of fifty-nine and a half. For example, if you determined that you can withdraw $8,500 the first year at age fifty-seven, then for each year in your five-year time frame until age sixty-two, you must take out the same $8,500.

There is a formula you need to figure the amount that is allowed for withdrawal. You only need three pieces of information to compute the amount. First, you must determine your estimated life expectancy. It can be found in the IRS Publication 590, Appendix C, which is available online. Thinking about how much time you have left may feel morbid, but it has to be done. It is also an opportunity to remind yourself that life is short and that you should make the most of each day. Next, you need to find the 120 percent midterm interest rate for your current month. It is published monthly and can be accessed at http://www.imagisoft.com/equal/ federalmidtermrates.html. You can use the interest rate of the current or preceding month. Finally, you simply need the most recent balance of your IRA or 401(k).

You have three methods to compute the amount. We will use only the amortization method because it gives you the largest amount compared with the other two methods. If you wish to learn about the other two methods or want more details about the 72(t) election, you can visit the IRS website at www.irs.gov.

With a business calculator, enter the three pieces of information: your estimated life expectancy, the 120 percent midterm rate, and the amount of your IRA or 401(k), which will determine the amount you can withdraw from your account.

If you do not have a business calculator or don't know how to use one, you can visit http://www.massmutual.com/mmcalcs/Retire72T.html, which is sponsored by Mass Mutual Financial Group. It has an easy-to-use

72(t) calculator. Instead of inputting the number of years you have remaining, simply enter your age, and the calculator will compute your life expectancy for you.

The yearly withdrawal amount may not be enough to fully finance your retirement, but it will help out, and you'll avoid paying a 10 percent penalty. Start the withdrawal the year after you leave your job, and you might avoid the higher tax bracket and save even more money.

This section on the 72(t) election is meant for the traditional IRA or 401(k). The rules are different if you have money in a Roth IRA. If your Roth IRA has been open for at least five years, you are allowed to take withdrawals limited to your original contributions without paying any income tax. However, if any earnings above your original contribution from the Roth IRA are taken out, then income tax will be due. In most cases, there is no early withdrawal penalty on the Roth IRA distribution. Check with a tax professional if you have any questions.

BIBLIOGRAPHY

"American Association for Long-Term Care." Accessed November 3, 2014. http://www.aaltci.org.

Corbett, Holly C. "5 Reasons to Take Your Teeth Seriously." *Prevention*, December 2011, http://www.prevention.com.

Cropp, Ian. "Why Do Hearing Aids Cost So Much?" *AARP*, October 3, 2014. http://www.aarp.org/health/conditions-treatments/info-05-2011/hearing-aids-cost.html

Dacyczyn, Amy. *The Complete Tightwad Gazette*. New York: Villard, 1998.

2014 Cost of Care Survey. Richmond, VA: Genworth Financial, 2014.

Hebner, Mark T. *Index Funds: The 12-Step Recovery Program for Active Investors*. Irvine, CA: IFA Publishing, 2013.

Jha, Prabhat, Chinthanie Ramasundarahettige, Victoria Landsman, Brian Rostron, Michael Thun, Robert N. Anderson, Tim McAfee, and Richard Peto. "21st-Century Hazards of Smoking and Benefits of Cessation in the United States." *The New England Journal of Medicine* 368, no. 4 (January 24, 2013): 341–350.

Jones, A. L., L. L. Dwyer, A. R. Bercovitz, and G. W. Strahan. "The National Nursing Home Survey: 2004 Overview." *Vital Health Statistics* 13, no. 167 (June 2009): 1–155.

Lasser, J. K. *J. K. Lasser's Your Income Tax 2015: For Preparing Your 2014 Tax Return*. Hoboken, NJ: John Wiley & Sons, 2014.

McGinley, Laurie. "Health Matters: The Next Wave of Medical Tourists Might Be You." *The Wall Street Journal*. Last modified February 16, 2008. http://www.wsj.com/articles/SB120283288380762505.

Vehicle Sustainability and Travel Mileage Schedules. Springfield, VA: National Highway Traffic Safety Administration, 2006.

Rhee, Nari. *The Retirement Savings Crisis: Is It Worse Than We Think?* Washington, DC: The National Institute on Retirement Security, June 2013.

Rumberger, Jill S., Christopher S. Hollenbeak, and David Kline. *Potential Costs and Benefits of Smoking Cessation: An Overview of the Approach to State Specific Analysis*. State College, PA: Pennsylvania State University, April 30, 2010.

Saad, Lydia. *Three in Four US Workers Plan to Work Past Retirement Age*. Princeton, NJ: Gallup Poll, 2013.

Swedroe, Larry E. *The Only Guide You'll Ever Need for the Right Financial Plan: Managing Your Wealth, Risk, and Investments*. New York: Bloomberg Press, 2010.

Consumer Expenditure Survey. Washington, DC: US Bureau of Labor Statistics, September 2014.

Wells, Bob. *How to Live in a Car, Van or RV*. Amazon Digital Services: 2012.

About the Authors

Randy Kirk and Jane Kirk, HIA, ALHC, are a husband-and-wife writing team of both fiction and nonfiction. Randy had a twenty-five-year career with the IRS, and Jane spent twenty-two years with a large national insurance company. They have successfully used many of the ideas in the book *Retired Broke* to secure their early retirement. They currently live in a Midwest suburb with Jane's eighty-five-year-old mother and their two aging cats.

We hope you found this book interesting and helpful.
Your fellow readers and we would appreciate it if you take a few minutes and write a review on Amazon.
Thank you for your honest feedback.

Made in the USA
Middletown, DE
30 July 2015